Preface

Microsoft Azure Database Administrator DP 300: Administering Relational Databases on Microsoft Azure is a comprehensive guide meticulously designed to equip database professionals with the expertise required to manage, monitor, and optimize Azure SQL Database environments. As cloud-based database solutions become integral to modern business operations, the role of a skilled database administrator has never been more crucial. This book aligns with the objectives of the DP-300 certification, covering key topics such as resource planning and implementation, security management, performance optimization, automation, and high availability strategies. Through a structured learning approach, it provides in-depth theoretical knowledge combined with real-world applications, ensuring a thorough understanding of Azure SQL Database administration principles and best practices.

Beyond certification preparation, Microsoft Certification DP-300: Administering Relational Databases on Microsoft Azure serves as a valuable reference for professionals aiming to refine their database management skills in cloud-based environments. Each chapter integrates practical exercises, detailed illustrations, expert insights, and self-assessment tools to reinforce conceptual understanding and technical proficiency. Additionally, online test papers and expert-led video tutorials further enhance the learning experience by bridging the gap between theoretical concepts and practical implementation. Whether you are an aspiring database administrator or an experienced professional looking to validate and expand your expertise, this book provides the essential knowledge and skills required to excel in Azure SQL Database administration and achieve success in cloud-based data management.

Table of Contents

Chapter 1: Practice Questions & Answers Part 1

QUESTION: 1

-

You have an Azure SQL Database managed instance named sqldbmi1 that contains a database name Sales. You need to initiate a backup of Sales.
How should you complete the Transact-SQL statement? To answer, select the appropriate options in the answer area.
NOTE: Each correct selection is worth one point.
A. Mastered
B. Not Mastered
Answer: A

QUESTION: 2

-

You have an Azure SQL Database server named sqlsrv1 that hosts 10 Azure SQL databases. The databases perform slower than expected.
You need to identify whether the performance issue relates to the use of tempdb on sqlsrv1. What should you do?
A. Run Query Store-based queries
B. Review information provided by SQL Server Profiler-based traces
C. Review information provided by Query Performance Insight
D. Run dynamic management view-based queries
Answer: D

QUESTION: 3

-

You are designing a date dimension table in an Azure Synapse Analytics dedicated SQL pool. The date dimension table will be used by all the fact tables.
Which distribution type should you recommend to minimize data movement?
A. HASH
B. REPLICATE
C. ROUND_ROBIN
Answer: B

QUESTION: 4

-

You have an Azure Data Lake Storage Gen2 account named account1 that stores logs as shown in the following table.
You do not expect that the logs will be accessed during the retention periods.
You need to recommend a solution for account1 that meets the following requirements:
Automatically deletes the logs at the end of each retention period
Minimizes storage costs
What should you include in the recommendation? To answer, select the appropriate options in the answer area.

NOTE: Each correct selection is worth one point.
A. Mastered
B. Not Mastered
Answer: A

QUESTION: 5
-
You have an Azure SQL database.
You discover that the plan cache is full of compiled plans that were used only once.
You run the select * from sys.database_scoped_configurations Transact-SQL command and receive the results shown in the following table.
You need relieve the memory pressure. What should you configure?
A. LEGACY_CARDINALITY_ESTIMATION
B. QUERY_OPTIMIZER_HOTFIXES
C. OPTIMIZE_FOR_AD_HOC_WORKLOADS
D. ACCELERATED_PLAN_FORCING
Answer: C

QUESTION: 6
-
You have a 50-TB Microsoft SQL Server database named DB1.
You need to reduce the time it takes to perform database consistency checks of DB1.
Which Transact-SQL command should you run? To answer, select the appropriate options in the answer area.
NOTE: Each correct selection is worth one point.
A. Mastered
B. Not Mastered
Answer: A

QUESTION: 7
-
You configure version control for an Azure Data Factory instance as shown in the following exhibit.

Use the drop-down menus to select the answer choice that completes each statement based on the information presented in the graphic.
NOTE: Each correct selection is worth one point.
A. Mastered
B. Not Mastered
Answer: A

QUESTION: 8
-
You are creating a managed data warehouse solution on Microsoft Azure.

You must use PolyBase to retrieve data from Azure Blob storage that resides in parquet format and load the data into a large table called FactSalesOrderDetails.
You need to configure Azure Synapse Analytics to receive the data.
Which four actions should you perform in sequence? To answer, move the appropriate actions from the list of actions to the answer area and arrange them in the
correct order.
A. Mastered
B. Not Mastered
Answer: A

QUESTION: 9

-

You have an Azure Databricks workspace named workspace1 in the Standard pricing tier. Workspace1 contains an all-purpose cluster named cluster1.
You need to reduce the time it takes for cluster1 to start and scale up. The solution must minimize costs. What should you do first?
A. Upgrade workspace1 to the Premium pricing tier.
B. Configure a global init script for workspace1.
C. Create a pool in workspace1.
D. Create a cluster policy in workspace1.
Answer: C

QUESTION: 10

-

You have an Azure subscription that is linked to an Azure AD tenant named contoso.com. The subscription contains an Azure SQL database named SQL 1 and an
Azure web named app1. App1 has the managed identity feature enabled. You need to create a new database user for app1.
How should you complete the Transact-SQL statement? To answer, select the appropriate options in the answer area.
NOTE: Each correct selection is worth one point.
A. Mastered
B. Not Mastered
Answer: A

QUESTION: 11

-

You are planning a solution that will use Azure SQL Database. Usage of the solution will peak from October 1 to January 1 each year.
During peak usage, the database will require the following:
24 cores
500 GB of storage
124 GB of memory
More than 50,000 IOPS
During periods of off-peak usage, the service tier of Azure SQL Database will be set to Standard.
Which service tier should you use during peak usage?

A. Business Critical
B. Premium
C. Hyperscale
Answer: A

QUESTION: 12

-

You have an Azure SQL database named DB1. You run a query while connected to DB1.
You review the actual execution plan for the query, and you add an index to a table referenced by the query. You need to compare the previous actual execution
plan for the query to the Live Query Statistics.
What should you do first in Microsoft SQL Server Management Studio (SSMS)?
A. For DB1, set QUERY_CAPTURE_MODE of Query Store to All.
B. Run the SET SHOWPLAN_ALL Transact-SQL statement.
C. Save the actual execution plan.
D. Enable Query Store for DB1.
Answer: C

QUESTION: 13

-

You have a new Azure SQL database. The database contains a column that stores confidential information. You need to track each time values from the column
are returned in a query. The tracking information must be stored for 365 days from the date the query was executed.
Which three actions should you perform? Each correct answer presents part of the solution.
NOTE: Each correct selection is worth one point.
A. Turn on auditing and write audit logs to an Azure Storage account.

B. Add extended properties to the column.
C. Turn on Advanced Data Security for the Azure SQL server.
D. Apply sensitivity labels named Highly Confidential to the column.
E. Turn on Azure Advanced Threat Protection (ATP).
Answer: ACD

QUESTION: 14

-

You have the following Transact-SQL query.
Which column returned by the query represents the free space in each file?
A. ColumnA
B. ColumnB
C. ColumnC
D. ColumnD
Answer: C

QUESTION: 15

-

You plan to create a table in an Azure Synapse Analytics dedicated SQL pool.
Data in the table will be retained for five years. Once a year, data that is older than five years will be deleted. You need to ensure that the data is distributed evenly
across partitions. The solutions must minimize the
amount of time required to delete old data.
How should you complete the Transact-SQL statement? To answer, drag the appropriate values to the correct targets. Each value may be used once, more than
once, or not at all.
You may need to drag the split bar between panes or scroll to view content.
NOTE: Each correct selection is worth one point.
A. Mastered
B. Not Mastered
Answer: A

QUESTION: 16

-

You have SQL Server 2019 on an Azure virtual machine that runs Windows Server 2019. The virtual machine has 4 vCPUs and 28 GB of memory.
You scale up the virtual machine to 16 vCPUSs and 64 GB of memory. You need to provide the lowest latency for tempdb.
What is the total number of data files that tempdb should contain?
A. 2
B. 4
C. 8
D. 64
Answer: D

QUESTION: 17

-

You plan to build a structured streaming solution in Azure Databricks. The solution will count new events in fiveminute intervals and report only events that arrive
during the interval.
The output will be sent to a Delta Lake table. Which output mode should you use?
A. complete
B. append
C. update
Answer: A

QUESTION: 18

-

You have an Azure SQL database that contains a table named Customer. Customer has the columns shown in the following table.
You plan to implement a dynamic data mask for the Customer_Phone column. The mask must meet the following requirements:

The first six numerals of each customer's phone number must be masked.
The last four digits of each customer's phone number must be visible.
Hyphens must be preserved and displayed.
How should you configure the dynamic data mask? To answer, select the appropriate options in the answer area.
A. Mastered
B. Not Mastered
Answer: A

QUESTION: 19

-

You are building a database in an Azure Synapse Analytics serverless SQL pool. You have data stored in Parquet files in an Azure Data Lake Storage Gen2
container. Records are structured as shown in the following sample.
The records contain two applicants at most.
You need to build a table that includes only the address fields.
How should you complete the Transact-SQL statement? To answer, select the appropriate options in the answer area.
NOTE: Each correct selection is worth one point.

A. Mastered
B. Not Mastered
Answer: A

QUESTION: 20

-

From a website analytics system, you receive data extracts about user interactions such as downloads, link clicks, form submissions, and video plays.
The data contains the following columns:
You need to design a star schema to support analytical queries of the data. The star schema will contain four tables including a date dimension.
To which table should you add each column? To answer, select the appropriate options in the answer area.
NOTE: Each correct selection is worth one point.

A. Mastered
B. Not Mastered
Answer: A

QUESTION: 21

-

You have an Azure data solution that contains an enterprise data warehouse in Azure Synapse Analytics named DW1.
Several users execute adhoc queries to DW1 concurrently. You regularly perform automated data loads to DW1.
You need to ensure that the automated data loads have enough memory available to complete quickly and successfully when the adhoc queries run.
What should you do?
A. Assign a smaller resource class to the automated data load queries.
B. Create sampled statistics to every column in each table of DW1.
C. Assign a larger resource class to the automated data load queries.
D. Hash distribute the large fact tables in DW1 before performing the automated data loads.
Answer: C

QUESTION: 22

-

You are developing an application that uses Azure Data Lake Storage Gen 2.
You need to recommend a solution to grant permissions to a specific application for a limited time period. What should you include in the recommendation?
A. role assignments
B. account keys
C. shared access signatures (SAS)
D. Azure Active Directory (Azure AD) identities
Answer: C

QUESTION: 23

-

You deploy a database to an Azure SQL Database managed instance.
You need to prevent read queries from blocking queries that are trying to write to the database.
Which database option should set?
A. PARAMETERIZATION to FORCED
B. PARAMETERIZATION to SIMPLE
C. Delayed Durability to Forced
D. READ_COMMITTED_SNAPSHOT to ON
Answer: D

QUESTION: 24

-

You have an Azure subscription.
You plan to deploy an Azure SQL database by using an Azure Resource Manager template.
How should you complete the template? To answer, select the appropriate options in the answer area.
NOTE: Each correct selection is worth one point.
A. Mastered
B. Not Mastered

QUESTION: 25

-
You have SQL Server on an Azure virtual machine that contains a database named DB1.
You view a plan summary that shows the duration in milliseconds of each execution of query 1178902 as shown in the following exhibit:
What should you do to ensure that the query uses the execution plan which executes in the least amount of time?
A. Force the query execution plan for plan 1221065.
B. Run the DBCC FREEPROCCACHE command.
C. Force the query execution plan for plan 1220917.
D. Disable parameter sniffing.
Answer: C

QUESTION: 26
-
You have a Microsoft SQL Server database named DB1 that contains a table named Table1. The database role membership for a user named User1 is shown in
the following exhibit.

Use the drop-down menus to select the answer choice that completes each statement based on the information presented in the graphic.
NOTE: Each correct selection is worth one point.
A. Mastered
B. Not Mastered
Answer: A

QUESTION: 27
-
A data engineer creates a table to store employee information for a new application. All employee names are in the US English alphabet. All addresses are
locations in the United States. The data engineer uses the following statement to create the table.

You need to recommend changes to the data types to reduce storage and improve performance. Which two actions should you recommend? Each correct answer
presents part of the solution. NOTE: Each correct selection is worth one point.
A. Change Salary to the money data type.
B. Change PhoneNumber to the float data type.
C. Change LastHireDate to the datetime2(7) data type.
D. Change PhoneNumber to the bigint data type.
E. Change LastHireDate to the date data type.
Answer: AE

QUESTION: 28

-
Note: This question is part of a series of questions that present the same scenario. Each question in the series contains a unique solution that might meet the
stated goals. Some question sets might have more than one correct solution, while others might not have a correct solution.
After you answer a question in this section, you will NOT be able to return to it. As a result, these questions will not appear in the review screen.
You have an Azure Data Lake Storage account that contains a staging zone.
You need to design a daily process to ingest incremental data from the staging zone, transform the data by executing an R script, and then insert the transformed
data into a data warehouse in Azure Synapse Analytics.
Solution: You use an Azure Data Factory schedule trigger to execute a pipeline that executes mapping data flow, and then inserts the data into the data
warehouse.
Does this meet the goal?
A. Yes
B. No
Answer: B

QUESTION: 29

-
You plan to deploy an app that includes an Azure SQL database and an Azure web app. The app has the following requirements:
The web app must be hosted on an Azure virtual network.
The Azure SQL database must be assigned a private IP address.
The Azure SQL database must allow connections only from the virtual network.
You need to recommend a solution that meets the requirements. What should you include in the recommendation?
A. Azure Private Link
B. a network security group (NSG)
C. a database-level firewall
D. a server-level firewall
Answer: A

QUESTION: 30

-
You have an Azure subscription that contains an Azure Data Factory version 2 (V2) data factory named df1. DF1 contains a linked service.
You have an Azure Key vault named vault1 that contains an encryption kay named key1. You need to encrypt df1 by using key1.
What should you do first?
A. Disable purge protection on vault1.
B. Remove the linked service from df1.
C. Create a self-hosted integration runtime.
D. Disable soft delete on vault1.
Answer: B

QUESTION: 31

-

You have the following Azure Resource Manager template.
For each of the following statements, select Yes if the statement is true. Otherwise, select No.
NOTE: Each correct selection is worth one point.
A. Mastered
B. Not Mastered
Answer: A

QUESTION: 32

-

You have an Azure Databricks resource.
You need to log actions that relate to changes in compute for the Databricks resource. Which Databricks services should you log?
A. clusters
B. jobs
C. DBFS
D. SSH
E. workspace
Answer: E

QUESTION: 33

-

You have SQL Server 2019 on an Azure virtual machine that contains an SSISDB database. A recent failure causes the master database to be lost.
You discover that all Microsoft SQL Server integration Services (SSIS) packages fail to run on the virtual machine.
Which four actions should you perform in sequence to resolve the issue? To answer, move the appropriate actions from the list of actions to the answer area and
arrange them in the correct.
A. Mastered
B. Not Mastered
Answer: A

QUESTION: 34

-

Note: This question is part of a series of questions that present the same scenario. Each question in the series contains a unique solution that might meet the
stated goals. Some question sets might have more than one correct solution, while others might not have a correct solution.
After you answer a question in this section, you will NOT be able to return to it. As a result, these questions will not appear in the review screen.
You have an Azure Synapse Analytics dedicated SQL pool that contains a table named Table1. You have files that are ingested and loaded into an Azure Data
Lake Storage Gen2 container named

container1.
You plan to insert data from the files into Table1 and transform the data. Each row of data in the files will produce one row in the serving layer of Table1.
You need to ensure that when the source data files are loaded to container1, the DateTime is stored as an additional column in Table1.
Solution: You use an Azure Synapse Analytics serverless SQL pool to create an external table that has an additional DateTime column.
Does this meet the goal?
A. Yes
B. No
Answer: A

QUESTION: 35

-
You need to trigger an Azure Data Factory pipeline when a file arrives in an Azure Data Lake Storage Gen2 container.
Which resource provider should you enable?
A. Microsoft.EventHub
B. Microsoft.EventGrid
C. Microsoft.Sql
D. Microsoft.Automation
Answer: B

QUESTION: 36

-
You have an on-premises Microsoft SQL Server 2016 server named Server1 that contains a database named DB1.
You need to perform an online migration of DB1 to an Azure SQL Database managed instance by using Azure Database Migration Service.
How should you configure the backup of DB1? To answer, select the appropriate options in the answer area. NOTE: Each correct selection is worth one point.
A. Mastered
B. Not Mastered
Answer: A

QUESTION: 37

-
You have an Azure Synapse Analytics dedicated SQL pool.
You run PDW_SHOWSPACEUSED('dbo.FactInternetSales'); and get the results shown in the following table.
Which statement accurately describes the dbo.FactInternetSales table?
A. The table contains less than 10,000 rows.
B. All distributions contain data.
C. The table uses round-robin distribution
D. The table is skewed.
Answer: D

QUESTION: 38

-

You are designing a dimension table in an Azure Synapse Analytics dedicated SQL pool.
You need to create a surrogate key for the table. The solution must provide the fastest query performance. What should you use for the surrogate key?

A. an IDENTITY column
B. a GUID column
C. a sequence object

Answer: A

QUESTION: 39

-

You have an Azure subscription that contains an Azure SQL managed instance named SQLMi1 and a SQL Agent job named Backupdb. Backupdb performs a
daily backup of the databases hosted on SQLMi1.
You need to be notified by email if the job fails.
Which three actions should you perform in sequence? To answer, move the appropriate actions from the list of actions to the answer area and arrange them in the
correct order.
NOTE: More than one order of answer choices is correct. You will receive credit for any of the correct orders you select.

A. Mastered
B. Not Mastered

Answer: A

QUESTION: 40

-

You have a new Azure subscription.
You create an Azure SQL Database instance named DB1 on an Azure SQL Database server named Server1. You need to ensure that users can connect to DB1
in the event of an Azure regional outage. In the event of an outage, applications that connect to DB1 must be able to connect without having to update the
connection
strings.
Which two actions should you perform? Each correct answer presents part of the solution.
NOTE: Each correct selection is worth one point.

A. From the properties of DB1. configure geo-replication.
B. From the properties of Server1 add a failover group.
C. Create a new Azure SQL Database server named Server2.
D. From the properties of Server1 configure retention for DB1
E. Create a new Azure SQL Database instance named DB2.

Answer: BC

QUESTION: 41

-

You have an Azure Active Directory (Azure AD) tenant named contoso.com that contains a user named user1@contoso.com and an Azure SQL managed instance named SQLMI1.

You need to ensure that user1@contoso.com can create logins in SQLMI1 that map to Azure AD service principals.

Which three actions should you perform in sequence? To answer, move the appropriate actions from the list of actions to the answer area and arrange them in the correct order.

A. Mastered

B. Not Mastered

Answer: A

QUESTION: 42

-

You have SQL Server on an Azure virtual machine.

You need to add a 4-TB volume that meets the following requirements:

Maximizes IOPs

Uses premium solid state drives (SSDs)

What should you do?

A. Attach two mirrored 4-TB SSDs.

B. Attach a stripe set that contains four 1-TB SSDs.

C. Attach a RAID-5 array that contains five 1-TB SSDs.

D. Attach a single 4-TB SSD.

Answer: B

QUESTION: 43

-

You need to recommend an availability strategy for an Azure SQL database. The strategy must meet the following requirements:

Support failovers that do not require client applications to change their connection strings.

Replicate the database to a secondary Azure region.

Support failover to the secondary region. What should you include in the recommendation?

A. failover groups

B. transactional replication

C. Availability Zones

D. geo-replication

Answer: A

QUESTION: 44

-

You have SQL Server on an Azure virtual machine that contains a database named DB1. You have an application that queries DB1 to generate a sales report.
You need to see the parameter values from the last time the query was executed.
Which two actions should you perform? Each correct answer presents part of the solution.
NOTE: Each correct selection is worth one point.
A. Enable Last_Query_Plan_Stats in the master database
B. Enable Lightweight_Query_Profiling in DB1
C. Enable Last_Query_Plan_Stats in DB1
D. Enable Lightweight_Query_Profiling in the master database
E. Enable PARAMETER_SNIFFING in DB1
Answer: AC

QUESTION: 45

-
Your company analyzes images from security cameras and sends alerts to security teams that respond to unusual activity. The solution uses Azure Databricks.
You need to send Apache Spark level events, Spark Structured Streaming metrics, and application metrics to Azure Monitor.
Which three actions should you perform in sequence? To answer, move the appropriate actions from the list of actions in the answer area and arrange them in the

correct order.
A. Mastered
B. Not Mastered
Answer: A

QUESTION: 46

-
You plan to develop a dataset named Purchases by using Azure Databricks. Purchases will contain the following columns:
ProductID
ItemPrice
LineTotal
Quantity
StoreID
Minute
Month
Hour
Year
Day
You need to store the data to support hourly incremental load pipelines that will vary for each StoreID. The solution must minimize storage costs.
How should you complete the code? To answer, select the appropriate options in the answer area.
NOTE: Each correct selection is worth one point.

A. Mastered

B. Not Mastered
Answer: A

QUESTION: 47
-
You have 40 Azure SQL databases, each for a different customer. All the databases reside on the same Azure SQL Database server.
You need to ensure that each customer can only connect to and access their respective database.
Which two actions should you perform? Each correct answer
presents part of the solution. NOTE: Each correct selection is worth one point.
A. Implement row-level security (RLS).
B. Create users in each database.
C. Configure the database firewall.
D. Configure the server firewall.
E. Create logins in the master database.
F. Implement Always Encrypted.
Answer: BC

QUESTION: 48
-
You are designing an enterprise data warehouse in Azure Synapse Analytics that will contain a table named Customers. Customers will contain credit card
information.
You need to recommend a solution to provide salespeople with the ability to view all the entries in Customers. The solution must prevent all the salespeople from
viewing or inferring the credit card information.
What should you include in the recommendation?
A. row-level security
B. data masking
C. Always Encrypted
D. column-level security
Answer: B

QUESTION: 49
-
You plan to move two 100-GB databases to Azure.
You need to dynamically scale resources consumption based on workloads. The solution must minimize downtime during scaling operations.
What should you use?
A. An Azure SQL Database elastic pool
B. SQL Server on Azure virtual machines
C. an Azure SQL Database managed instance

D. Azure SQL databases
Answer: A

QUESTION: 50

-

Note: This question is part of a series of questions that present the same scenario. Each question in the series contains a unique solution that might meet the
stated goals. Some question sets might have more than one correct solution, while others might not have a correct solution.
After you answer a question in this section, you will NOT be able to return to it. As a result, these questions will not appear in the review screen.
You have SQL Server 2019 on an Azure virtual machine.
You are troubleshooting performance issues for a query in a SQL Server instance.
To gather more information, you query sys.dm_exec_requests and discover that the wait type is PAGELATCH_UP and the wait_resource is 2:3:905856.
You need to improve system performance.
Solution: You change the data file for the master database to autogrow by 10 percent. Does this meet the goal?
A. Yes
B. No
Answer: B

QUESTION: 51

-

You are designing a streaming data solution that will ingest variable volumes of data. You need to ensure that you can change the partition count after creation.
Which service should you use to ingest the data?
A. Azure Event Hubs Standard
B. Azure Stream Analytics
C. Azure Data Factory
D. Azure Event Hubs Dedicated
Answer: D

QUESTION: 52

-

You are planning disaster recovery for the failover group of an Azure SQL Database managed instance.
Your company's SLA requires that the database in the failover group become available as quickly as possible if a major outage occurs.
You set the Read/Write failover policy to Automatic.
What are two results of the configuration? Each correct answer presents a complete solution.
NOTE: Each correct selection is worth one point.
A. In the event of a datacenter or Azure regional outage, the databases will fail over automatically.
B. In the event of an outage, the databases in the primary instance will fail over immediately.
C. In the event of an outage, you can selectively fail over individual databases.
D. In the event of an outage, you can set a different grace period to fail over each database.

E. In the event of an outage, the minimum delay for the databases to fail over in the primary instance will be one hour.
Answer: AE

QUESTION: 53

-

You need to migrate an on-premises Microsoft SQL Server database to Azure SQL Database. The solution must minimize downtime.
What should you do?
A. Configure Transaction Log Shipping.
B. Implement Always On availability groups.
C. Configure transactional replication.
D. Import a BACPAC.
Answer: C

QUESTION: 54

-

Note: This question is part of a series of questions that present the same scenario. Each question in the series contains a unique solution that might meet the stated goals. Some question sets might have more than one correct solution, while others might not have a correct solution.
After you answer a question in this section, you will NOT be able to return to it. As a result, these questions will not appear in the review screen.
You have two Azure SQL Database servers named Server1 and Server2. Each server contains an Azure SQL database named Database1.
You need to restore Database1 from Server1 to Server2. The solution must replace the existing Database1 on Server2.
Solution: You run the Remove-AzSqlDatabase PowerShell cmdlet for Database1 on Server2. You run the Restore-AzSqlDatabase PowerShell cmdlet for Database1 on Server2.

Does this meet the goal?
A. Yes
B. No
Answer: B

QUESTION: 55

-

Note: This question is part of a series of questions that present the same scenario. Each question in the series contains a unique solution that might meet the stated goals. Some question sets might have more than one correct solution, while others might not have a correct solution.
After you answer a question in this section, you will NOT be able to return to it. As a result, these questions will not appear in the review screen.

You have an Azure SQL database named Sales.
You need to implement disaster recovery for Sales to meet the following requirements:
During normal operations, provide at least two readable copies of Sales.
Ensure that Sales remains available if a datacenter fails.
Solution: You deploy an Azure SQL database that uses the General Purpose service tier and failover groups. Does this meet the goal?
A. Yes
B. No
Answer: B

QUESTION: 56

-

You have an Azure SQL database.
Users report that the executions of a stored procedure are slower than usual. You suspect that a regressed query is causing the performance issue.
You need to view the query execution plan to verify whether a regressed query is causing the issue. The solution must minimize effort.
What should you use?
A. Performance Recommendations in the Azure portal
B. Extended Events in Microsoft SQL Server Management Studio (SSMS)
C. Query Store in Microsoft SQL Server Management Studio (SSMS)
D. Query Performance Insight in the Azure portal
Answer: C

QUESTION: 57

-

You are designing an anomaly detection solution for streaming data from an Azure IoT hub. The solution must meet the following requirements:
Send the output to an Azure Synapse.
Identify spikes and dips in time series data.
Minimize development and configuration effort. Which should you include in the solution?
A. Azure SQL Database
B. Azure Databricks
C. Azure Stream Analytics
Answer: C

QUESTION: 58

-

You have an Azure Stream Analytics job.
You need to ensure that the job has enough streaming units provisioned. You configure monitoring of the SU % Utilization metric.
Which two additional metrics should you monitor? Each correct answer presents part of the solution. NOTE: Each correct selection is worth one point.
A. Late Input Events
B. Out of order Events
C. Backlogged Input Events

D. Watermark Delay
E. Function Events
Answer: CD

QUESTION: 59

-

Note: This question is part of a series of questions that present the same scenario. Each question in the series contains a unique solution that might meet the
stated goals. Some question sets might have more than one correct solution, while others might not have a correct solution.
After you answer a question in this section, you will NOT be able to return to it. As a result, these questions will not appear in the review screen.
You have an Azure Data Lake Storage account that contains a staging zone.
You need to design a daily process to ingest incremental data from the staging zone, transform the data by executing an R script, and then insert the transformed
data into a data warehouse in Azure Synapse Analytics.
Solution: You use an Azure Data Factory schedule trigger to execute a pipeline that copies the data to a staging table in the data warehouse, and then uses a
stored procedure to execute the R script.
Does this meet the goal?
A. Yes
B. No
Answer: A

QUESTION: 60

-

You have an Azure SQL database named DBI that contains a nonclustered index named index1. End users report slow queries when they use index1.
You need to identify the operations that are being performed on the index. Which dynamic management view should you use?
A. Option A
B. Option B
C. Option C
D. Option D
Answer: D

QUESTION: 61

-

You have an Azure SQL managed instance.
You need to enable SQL Agent Job email notifications. What should you do?
A. Use the Agent XPs option.
B. Enable the SQL Server Agent.
C. Run the sp_configure command.

D. Run the sp set_agent properties command.
Answer: C

QUESTION: 62

-

You are performing exploratory analysis of bus fare data in an Azure Data Lake Storage Gen2 account by using an Azure Synapse Analytics serverless SQL pool.
You execute the Transact-SQL query shown in the following exhibit.
Use the drop-down menus to select the answer choice that completes each statement based on the information presented in the graphic.
A. Mastered
B. Not Mastered
Answer: A

QUESTION: 63

-

You are creating a new notebook in Azure Databricks that will support R as the primary language but will also support Scala and SQL.
Which switch should you use to switch between languages?
A. \\[<language>]
B. %<language>
C. \\[<language>]
D. @<language>
Answer: B

QUESTION: 64

-

You have an Azure Data Factory that contains 10 pipelines.
You need to label each pipeline with its main purpose of either ingest, transform, or load. The labels must be available for grouping and filtering when using the
monitoring experience in Data Factory.
What should you add to each pipeline?
A. an annotation
B. a resource tag
C. a run group ID
D. a user property
E. a correlation ID
Answer: A

QUESTION: 65

-

You have a Microsoft SQL Server 2017 server.
You need to migrate the server to Azure. The solution must meet the following requirements:
• Ensure that the latest version of SQL Server is used.
• Support the SQL Server Agent service. Minimize administrative effort.
What should you use?

A. SQL Server on Azure Virtual Machines
B. Azure SQL Database
C. an Azure SQL Database elastic pool
D. Azure SQL Managed Instance
Answer: A

QUESTION: 66

-

You have a version-8.0 Azure Database for MySQL database.
You need to identify which database queries consume the most resources. Which tool should you use?
A. Query Store
B. Metrics
C. Query Performance Insight
D. Alerts
Answer: A

QUESTION: 67

-

You have an Azure Synapse Analytics dedicated SQL pool named Pool1 and an Azure Data Lake Storage Gen2 account named Account1.
You plan to access the files in Account1 by using an external table.
You need to create a data source in Pool1 that you can reference when you create the external table.
How should you complete the Transact-SQL statement? To
answer, select the appropriate options in the
answer area.
NOTE: Each correct selection is worth one point.

A. Mastered
B. Not Mastered
Answer: A

QUESTION: 68

-

You have the following Azure Data Factory pipelines:
Ingest Data from System1
Ingest Data from System2
Populate Dimensions
Populate Facts
Ingest Data from System1 and Ingest Data from System2 have no dependencies. Populate Dimensions must execute after Ingest Data from System1 and Ingest
Data from System2. Populate Facts must execute after the Populate Dimensions pipeline. All the pipelines must execute every eight hours.
What should you do to schedule the pipelines for execution?

A. Add a schedule trigger to all four pipelines.
B. Add an event trigger to all four pipelines.
C. Create a parent pipeline that contains the four pipelines and use an event trigger.
D. Create a parent pipeline that contains the four pipelines and use a schedule trigger.
Answer: D

QUESTION: 69

-

You have an Azure subscription that contains an Azure SQL database named SQL1. SQL1 is in an Azure region that does not support availability zones.
You need to ensure that you have a secondary replica of SQLI in the same region. What should you use?
A. log shipping
B. auto-failover groups
C. active geo-replication
D. Microsoft SQL Server failover clusters
Answer: C

QUESTION: 70

-

You have an Azure SQL Database managed instance. The instance starts experiencing performance issues.
You need to identify which query is causing the issue and retrieve the execution plan for the query. The solution must minimize administrative effort.
What should you use?
A. the Azure portal
B. Extended Events
C. Query Store
D. dynamic management views
Answer: C

QUESTION: 71

- You have an Azure SQL database. You identify a long running query.
You need to identify which operation in the query is causing the performance issue.
What should you use to display the query execution plan in Microsoft SQL Server Management Studio (SSMS)?
A. Live Query Statistics
B. an estimated execution plan
C. an actual execution plan
D. Client Statistics
Answer: C

QUESTION: 72

-

You have an on-premises Microsoft SQL Server 2019 instance that hosts a database named DB1.

You plan to perform an online migration of DB1 to an Azure SQL managed instance by using the Azure Database Migration Service.
You need to create a backup of DB1 that is accessible to the Azure Database Migration Service.
What should you run for the backup and where should you store the backup? To answer, select the appropriate options in the answer area.
NOTE: Each correct selection is worth one point.
A. Mastered
B. Not Mastered
Answer: A

QUESTION: 73

-

You have an Azure subscription that contains the resources shown in the following table.
You need to back up db1 to mysqlbackups, and then restore the backup to a new database named db2 that is hosted on SQL1. The solution must ensure that db1
is backed up to a stripe set.
Which three Transact-SQL statements should you execute in sequence? To answer, move the appropriate statements from the list of statements to the answer
area and arrange them in the correct order.
A. Mastered
B. Not Mastered
Answer: A

QUESTION: 74

-

You have an Azure virtual machine named VM1 on a virtual network named VNet1. Outbound traffic from VM1 to the internet is blocked.
You have an Azure SQL database named SqlDb1 on a logical server named SqlSrv1.
You need to implement connectivity between VM1 and SqlDb1 to meet the following requirements:
Restrict network connectivity to SqlSrv1.
What should you create on VNet1?
A. a VPN gateway
B. a service endpoint
C. a private endpoint
D. an ExpressRoute gateway
Answer: C

QUESTION: 75

-

You have a resource group named App1Dev that contains an Azure SQL Database server named DevServer1. DevServer1 contains an Azure SQL database
named DB1. The schema and permissions for DB1 are saved in a Microsoft SQL Server Data Tools (SSDT) database project.
You need to populate a new resource group named App1Test with the DB1 database and an Azure SQL Server named TestServer1. The resources in App1Test

must have the same configurations as the resources in App1Dev.
Which four actions should you perform in sequence? To answer, move the appropriate actions from the list of actions to the answer area and arrange them in the
correct order.
A. Mastered
B. Not Mastered
Answer: A

QUESTION: 76

-

You have an Azure SQL database named DB1 that contains a private certificate named Sales. The private key for Sales is encrypted with a password. You need
to change the password for the private key. Which
Transact-SQL statement should you run?
A)
B)
C)
D)
A. Option A
B. Option B
C. Option C
D. Option D
Answer: C

QUESTION: 77

-

You create five Azure SQL Database instances on the same logical server.
In each database, you create a user for an Azure Active Directory (Azure AD) user named User1.
User1 attempts to connect to the logical server by using Azure
Data Studio and receives a login error.
You need to ensure that when User1 connects to the logical server by using Azure Data Studio, User1 can see all the databases.
What should you do?
A. Create User1 in the master database.
B. Assign User1 the db_datareader role for the master database.
C. Assign User1 the db_datareader role for the databases that Userl creates.
D. Grant select on sys.databases to public in the master database.
Answer: A

QUESTION: 78

-

You have an Azure SQL database that contains a table named Employees. Employees contains a column named Salary.
You need to encrypt the Salary column. The solution must prevent database administrators from reading the data in the Salary column and must provide the most
secure encryption.

Which three actions should you perform in sequence? To answer, move the appropriate actions from the list of actions to the answer area and arrange them in the correct order.
A. Mastered
B. Not Mastered
Answer: A

QUESTION: 79
-
Note: This question is part of a series of questions that present the same scenario. Each question in the series contains a unique solution that might meet the stated goals. Some question sets might have more than one correct solution, while others might not have a correct solution.
After you answer a question in this section, you will NOT be able to return to it. As a result, these questions will not appear in the review screen.
You have an Azure SQL database named Sales.
You need to implement disaster recovery for Sales to meet the following requirements:
 During normal operations, provide at least two readable copies of Sales.
 Ensure that Sales remains available if a datacenter fails.
Solution: You deploy an Azure SQL database that uses the General Purpose service tier and geo-replication. Does this meet the goal?
A. Yes
B. No
Answer: B

QUESTION: 80
-
You have an Azure SQL database named DB1.
You need to ensure that DB1 will support automatic failover without data loss if a datacenter fails. The solution must minimize costs.
Which deployment option and pricing tier should you configure?
A. Azure SQL Database Premium
B. Azure SQL Database serverless
C. Azure SQL Database managed instance Business Critical
D. Azure SQL Database Standard
Answer: A

QUESTION: 81
-
You have an Azure Data Factory pipeline that performs an incremental load of source data to an Azure Data Lake Storage Gen2 account.
Data to be loaded is identified by a column named LastUpdatedDate in the source table. You plan to execute the pipeline every four hours.

You need to ensure that the pipeline execution meets the following requirements:
Automatically retries the execution when the pipeline run fails due to concurrency or throttling limits. Supports backfilling existing data in the table.
Which type of trigger should you use?
A. tumbling window
B. on-demand
C. event
D. schedule
Answer: A

QUESTION: 82
-
You have an Azure SQL managed instance named SQLMI1 that has Resource Governor enabled and is used by two apps named App1 and App2.
You need to configure SQLMI1 to limit the CPU and memory resources that can be allocated to App1. Which four actions should you perform in sequence? To
answer, move the appropriate actions from the list of actions to the answer area and arrange them in the correct order.
A. Mastered
B. Not Mastered
Answer: A

QUESTION: 83
-
Note: This question is part of a series of questions that present the same scenario. Each question in the series contains a unique solution that might meet the
stated goals. Some question sets might have more than one correct solution, while others might not have a correct solution.
After you answer a question in this section, you will NOT be able to return to it. As a result, these questions will not appear in the review screen.
You have two Azure SQL Database servers named Server1 and Server2. Each server contains an Azure SQL database named Database1.
You need to restore Database1 from Server1 to Server2. The solution must replace the existing Database1 on Server2.
Solution: From the Azure portal, you delete Database1 from Server2, and then you create a new database on Server2 by using the backup of Database1 from
Server1.

Does this meet the goal?
A. Yes
B. No
Answer: B

QUESTION: 84

-

You have an Azure SQL database named db1 that contains an Azure Active Directory (Azure AD) user named user1.

You need to test impersonation of user1 in db1 by running a SELECT statement and returning to the original execution context.

How should you complete the Transact-SQL statement? To answer, select the appropriate options in the answer area.

NOTE: Each correct selection is worth one point.

A. Mastered

B. Not Mastered

Answer: A

QUESTION: 85

-

You have an Azure SQL managed instance named SQLMI1 that hosts 10 databases.

You need to implement alerts by using Azure Monitor. The solution must meet the following requirements: Minimize costs.

Aggregate Intelligent Insights telemetry from each database. What should you do?

A. From the Diagnostic settings of each database, select Send to Log Analytics.

B. From the Diagnostic settings of each database, select Stream to an event hub.

C. From the Diagnostic settings of SQLMI1. select Send to Log Analytics.

D. From the Diagnostic settings of SQLMI1. select Stream to an event hub.

Answer: A

QUESTION: 86

-

Note: This question is part of a series of questions that present the same scenario. Each question in the series contains a unique solution that might meet the stated goals. Some question sets might have more than one correct solution, while others might not have a correct solution.

After you answer a question in this section, you will NOT be able to return to it. As a result, these questions will not appear in the review screen.

You have SQL Server 2019 on an Azure virtual machine.

You are troubleshooting performance issues for a query in a SQL Server instance.

To gather more information, you query sys.dm_exec_requests and discover that the wait type is PAGELATCH_UP and the wait_resource is 2:3:905856.

You need to improve system performance.

Solution: You reduce the use of table variables and temporary tables. Does this meet the goal?

A. Yes

B. No

Answer: A

QUESTION: 87

-

You have an Azure subscription that contains the resources shown in the following table.

App1 experiences transient connection errors and timeouts when it attempts to access db1 after extended periods of inactivity. You need to modify db1 to resolve
the issues experienced by App1 as soon as possible, without considering immediate costs. What should you do?
A. Increase the number Of vCores allocated to db1.
B. Disable auto-pause delay for dbl.
C. Decrease the auto-pause delay for db1.
D. Enable automatic tuning for db1.
Answer: D

QUESTION: 88

-

You have an Azure SQL database.
You have a query and the associated execution plan as shown in the following exhibit.
Use the drop-down menus to select the answer choice that completes each statement based on the information presented in the graphic.
NOTE: Each correct selection is worth one point.
A. Mastered
B. Not Mastered
Answer: A

QUESTION: 89

-

You have an Azure data factory that has two pipelines named PipelineA and PipelineB. PipelineA has four activities as shown in the following exhibit.
PipelineB has two activities as shown in the following exhibit.
You create an alert for the data factory that uses Failed pipeline runs metrics for both pipelines and all failure types. The metric has the following settings:
Operator: Greater than
Aggregation type: Total
Threshold value: 2
Aggregation granularity (Period): 5 minutes
Frequency of evaluation: Every 5 minutes
Data Factory monitoring records the failures shown in the following table.
For each of the following statements, select Yes if the statement is true. Otherwise, select No.
NOTE: Each correct selection is worth one point.
A. Mastered
B. Not Mastered
Answer: A

QUESTION: 90

-

You have a SQL Server on Azure Virtual Machines instance that hosts a database named Db1. You need to configure the autogrow and autoshrink settings for
DB1.

Which statements should you use? To answer, select the appropriate options in the answer area.
NOTE: Each correct selection is worth one point.

A. Mastered
B. Not Mastered
Answer: A

QUESTION: 91

-

You have an Azure subscription that contains the resources shown in the following table.
You need to create a read-only replica of DB1 and configure the App1 instances to use the replica.
What should you do? To answer, select the appropriate options in the answer area.
NOTE: Each correct selection is worth one point.
A. Mastered
B. Not Mastered
Answer: A

QUESTION: 92

-

You have an Azure virtual machine named VM1 on a virtual network named VNet1. Outbound traffic from VM1 to the internet is blocked.
You have an Azure SQL database named SqlDb1 on a logical server named SqlSrv1.
You need to implement connectivity between VM1 and SqlDb1 to meet the following requirements:
 Ensure that all traffic to the public endpoint of SqlSrv1 is blocked.
 Minimize the possibility of VM1 exfiltrating data stored in SqlDb1. What should you create on VNet1?
A. a VPN gateway
B. a service endpoint
C. a private link
D. an ExpressRoute gateway
Answer: C

QUESTION: 93

-

You have an Azure SQL database named DB3.
You need to provide a user named DevUser with the ability to view the properties of DB3 from Microsoft SQL Server Management Studio (SSMS) as shown in the exhibit. (Click the Exhibit tab.)
Which Transact-SQL command should you run?
A. GRANT SHOWPLAN TO DevUser
B. GRANT VIEW DEFINITION TO DevUser
C. GRANT VIEW DATABASE STATE TO DevUser
D. GRANT SELECT TO DevUser

Answer: C

QUESTION: 94

-

Note: This question is part of a series of questions that present the same scenario. Each question in the series contains a unique solution that might meet the
stated goals. Some question sets might have more than one correct solution, while others might not have a correct solution.
After you answer a question in this section, you will NOT be able to return to it. As a result, these questions will not appear in the review screen.
You have SQL Server 2019 on an Azure virtual machine.
You are troubleshooting performance issues for a query in a SQL Server instance.
To gather more information, you query sys.dm_exec_requests and discover that the wait type is PAGELATCH_UP and the wait_resource is 2:3:905856.
You need to improve system performance. Solution: You shrink the transaction log file. Does this meet the goal?
A. Yes
B. No
Answer: B

QUESTION: 95

-

You need to apply 20 built-in Azure Policy definitions to all new and existing Azure SQL Database deployments in an Azure subscription. The solution must
minimize administrative effort.
Which three actions should you perform in sequence? To answer, move the appropriate actions from the list of actions to the answer area and arrange them in the
correct order.
A. Mastered
B. Not Mastered
Answer: A

QUESTION: 96

-

Note: This question is part of a series of questions that present the same scenario. Each question in the series contains a unique solution that might meet the
stated goals. Some question sets might have more than one correct solution, while others might not have a correct solution.
After you answer a question in this section, you will NOT be able to return to it. As a result, these questions will not appear in the review screen.
You have an Azure Synapse Analytics dedicated SQL pool that contains a table named Table1. You have files that are ingested and loaded into an Azure Data
Lake Storage Gen2 container named
container1.
You plan to insert data from the files into Table1 and transform the data. Each row of data in the files will produce one row in the serving layer of Table1.

You need to ensure that when the source data files are loaded to container1, the DateTime is stored as an additional column in Table1.
Solution: You use a dedicated SQL pool to create an external table that has an additional DateTime column. Does this meet the goal?
A. Yes
B. No
Answer: B

QUESTION: 97

-

You have a SQL Server on Azure Virtual Machines instance named VM1 that hosts a database named DB1. You run the following query.
For each of the following statements, select Yes if the statement is true. Otherwise, select No.

A. Mastered
B. Not Mastered
Answer: A

QUESTION: 98

-

You have an Always On availability group deployed to Azure virtual machines. The availability group contains a database named DB1 and has two nodes named SQL1 and SQL2. SQL1 is the primary replica.
You need to initiate a full backup of DB1 on SQL2. Which statement should you run?
A. BACKUP DATABASE DB1 TO URL='https://mystorageaccount.blob.core.windows.net/mycontainer/DB1.bak' with (Differential, STATS=5, COMPRESSION);
B. BACKUP DATABASE DB1 TO URL='https://mystorageaccount.blob.core.windows.net/mycontainer/DB1.bak' with (COPY_ONLY, STATS=5, COMPRESSION);
C. BACKUP DATABASE DB1 TO URL='https://mystorageaccount.blob.core.windows.net/mycontainer/DB1.bak' with (File_Snapshot, STATS=5, COMPRESSION);
D. BACKUP DATABASE DB1 TO URL='https://mystorageaccount.blob.core.windows.net/mycontainer/DB1.bak' with (NoInit, STATS=5, COMPRESSION);
Answer: B

QUESTION: 99

-

You have an Azure SQL database named sqldb1.
You need to minimize the amount of space by the data and log files of sqldb1. What should you run?
A. DBCC SHRINKDATABASE
B. sp_clean_db_free_space
C. sp_clean_db_file_free_space
D. DBCC SHRINKFILE

Answer: A

QUESTION: 100

-

You have an Azure Data Lake Storage Gen2 container.

Data is ingested into the container, and then transformed by a data integration application. The data is NOT

modified after that. Users can read files in the container but cannot modify the files.

You need to design a data archiving solution that meets the following requirements:

New data is accessed frequently and must be available as quickly as possible.

Data that is older than five years is accessed infrequently but must be available within one second when requested.

Data that us older than seven years is NOT accessed. After seven years, the data must be persisted at the lowest cost possible.

Costs must be minimized while maintaining the required availability.

How should you manage the data? To answer, select the appropriate options in the answer area.

NOTE: Each correct selection is worth one point.

A. Mastered

B. Not Mastered

Answer: A

QUESTION: 101

-

You have two on-premises servers that run Windows Server 2019 and host a Microsoft SQL Server 2017 Always On availability group named AG1. AG1 contains

a single database named DB1.

You have an Azure subscription. The subscription contains a virtual machine named VM1 that runs Linux. You need to migrate DB1 to a SQL Server 2019

instance on VM1. The solution must minimize the downtime of DB1 during the migration.

What should you do? To answer, select the appropriate options in the answer area. NOTE: Each correct selection is worth one point.

A. Mastered

B. Not Mastered

Answer: A

Chapter 2: Practice Questions & Answers Part 2

QUESTION: 102
You have an Azure SQL managed instance.
You need to gather the last execution of a query plan and its runtime statistics. The solution must minimize the impact on currently running queries.
What should you do?
A. Generate an estimated execution plan.
B. Generate an actual execution plan.
C. Run sys.dm_exec_query_plan_scacs.
D. Generate Live Query Statistics.
Answer: C

QUESTION: 103
- (Exam Topic 4)
You need to design a data retention solution for the Twitter feed data records. The solution must meet the customer sentiment analytics requirements.
Which Azure Storage functionality should you include in the solution?
A. time-based retention
B. change feed
C. lifecycle management
D. soft delete
Answer: C

QUESTION: 104
- (Exam Topic 2)
You need to implement a solution to notify the administrators. The solution must meet the monitoring requirements.
What should you do?
A. Create an Azure Monitor alert rule that has a static threshold and assign the alert rule to an action group.
B. Add a diagnostic setting that logs QueryStoreRuntimeStatistics and streams to an Azure event hub.
C. Add a diagnostic setting that logs Timeouts and streams to an Azure event hub.
D. Create an Azure Monitor alert rule that has a dynamic threshold and assign the alert rule to an action group.
Answer: D

QUESTION: 105
- (Exam Topic 2)
What should you use to migrate the PostgreSQL database?
A. Azure Data Box
B. AzCopy
C. Azure Database Migration Service
D. Azure Site Recovery
Answer: C

QUESTION: 106
- (Exam Topic 2)
Based on the PaaS prototype, which Azure SQL Database compute tier should you use?
A. Business Critical 4-vCore
B. Hyperscale
C. General Purpose v-vCore
D. Serverless
Answer: A

QUESTION: 107
- (Exam Topic 1)
You are evaluating the business goals.
Which feature should you use to provide customers with the required level of access based on their service agreement?
A. dynamic data masking
B. Conditional Access in Azure
C. service principals
D. row-level security (RLS)
Answer: D

QUESTION: 108
- (Exam Topic 1)
You need to provide an implementation plan to configure data retention for ResearchDB1. The solution must meet the security and compliance requirements.
What should you include in the plan?
A. Configure the Deleted databases settings for ResearchSrvOL
B. Deploy and configure an Azure Backup server.
C. Configure the Advanced Data Security settings for ResearchDBL
D. Configure the Manage Backups settings for ResearchSrvOL
Answer: D

QUESTION: 109
- (Exam Topic 1)
You create all of the tables and views for ResearchDB1.
You need to implement security for ResearchDB1. The solution must meet the security and compliance requirements.
Which three actions should you perform in sequence? To answer, move the appropriate actions from the list of actions to the answer area and arrange them in the
correct order.
A. Mastered
B. Not Mastered
Answer: A

QUESTION: 110
- (Exam Topic 1)

You need to identify the cause of the performance issues on SalesSQLDb1.
Which two dynamic management views should you use? Each correct answer presents part of the solution.
NOTE: Each correct selection is worth one point.
A. sys.dm_pdw_nodes_tran_locks
B. sys.dm_exec_compute_node_errors
C. sys.dm_exec_requests
D. sys.dm_cdc_errors
E. sys.dm_pdw_nodes_os_wait_stats
F. sys.dm_tran_locks
Answer: AE

QUESTION: 112
You are planning disaster recovery for the failover group of an Azure SQL Database managed instance.
Your company's SLA requires that the database in the failover group become available as quickly as possible if a major outage occurs. You set the Read/Write
failover policy to Automatic.
What are two results of the configuration? Each correct answer presents a complete solution.
NOTE: Each correct selection is worth one point.
A. In the event of a datacenter or Azure regional outage, the databases will fail over automatically.
B. In the event of an outage, the databases in the primary instance will fail over immediately.
C. In the event of an outage, you can selectively fail over individual databases.
D. In the event of an outage, you can set a different grace period to fail over each database.
E. In the event of an outage, the minimum delay for the databases to fail over in the primary instance will be one hour.
Answer: AE

QUESTION: 113
Note: This question is part of a series of questions that present the same scenario. Each question in the series contains a unique solution that might meet the
stated goals. Some question sets might have more than one correct solution, while others might not have a correct solution.
After you answer a question in this section, you will NOT be able to return to it. As a result, these questions will not appear in the review screen.
You have an Azure SQL database named Sales.
You need to implement disaster recovery for Sales to meet the following requirements: During normal operations, provide at least two readable copies of Sales.
Ensure that Sales remains available if a datacenter fails.
Solution: You deploy an Azure SQL database that uses the General Purpose service tier and geo-replication. Does this meet the goal?
A. Yes
B. No
Answer: E

QUESTION: 114

Explanation:
1. You need to implement authentication for ResearchDB1. The solution must meet the security and compliance requirements.
What should you run as part of the implementation?
A. CREATE LOGIN and the FROM WINDOWS clause
B. CREATE USER and the FROM CERTIFICATE clause
C. CREATE USER and the FROM LOGIN clause
D. CREATE USER and the ASYMMETRIC KEY clause
E. CREATE USER and the FROM EXTERNAL PROVIDER clause

QUESTION: 115
You have an Azure SQL database named sqldb1.
You need to minimize the possibility of Query Store transitioning to a read-only state. What should you do?
A. Double the value of Data Flush interval
B. Decrease by half the value of Data Flush Interval
C. Double the value of Statistics Collection Interval
D. Decrease by half the value of Statistics Collection interval
Answer: B

QUESTION: 116
You have SQL Server 2019 on an Azure virtual machine that runs Windows Server 2019. The virtual machine has 4 vCPUs and 28 GB of memory. You scale up
the virtual machine to 16 vCPUSs and 64 GB of memory.
You need to provide the lowest latency for tempdb.
What is the total number of data files that tempdb should contain?
A. 2
B. 4
C. 8
D. 64
Answer: B

QUESTION: 117
You need to recommend an availability strategy for an Azure SQL database. The strategy must meet the following requirements: Support failovers that do not
require client applications to change their connection strings.
Replicate the database to a secondary Azure region. Support failover to the secondary region.
What should you include in the recommendation?
A. failover groups
B. transactional replication
C. Availability Zones
D. geo-replication
Answer: D

QUESTION: 118

You are building a database backup solution for a SQL Server database hosted on an Azure virtual machine.
In the event of an Azure regional outage, you need to be able to restore the database backups. The solution must minimize costs. Which type of storage accounts
should you use for the backups?
A. locally-redundant storage (LRS)
B. read-access geo-redundant storage (RA-GRS)
C. zone-redundant storage (ZRS)
D. geo-redundant storage
Answer: B

QUESTION: 119
You have SQL Server on Azure virtual machines in an availability group.
You have a database named DB1 that is NOT in the availability group. You create a full database backup of DB1.
You need to add DB1 to the availability group.
Which restore option should you use on the secondary replica?
A. Restore with Recovery
B. Restore with Norecovery
C. Restore with Standby
Answer: B

QUESTION: 120
You are planning disaster recovery for the failover group of an Azure SQL Database managed instance.
Your company's SLA requires that the database in the failover group become available as quickly as possible if a major outage occurs. You set the Read/Write
failover policy to Automatic.
What are two results of the configuration? Each correct answer presents a complete solution.
NOTE: Each correct selection is worth one point.
A. In the event of a datacenter or Azure regional outage, the databases will fail over automatically.
B. In the event of an outage, the databases in the primary instance will fail over immediately.
C. In the event of an outage, you can selectively fail over individual databases.
D. In the event of an outage, you can set a different grace period to fail over each database.
E. In the event of an outage, the minimum delay for the databases to fail over in the primary instance will be one hour.
Answer: AE

QUESTION: 122
-
You have an Azure SQL Database managed instance named sqldbmi1 that contains a database name Sales. You need to initiate a backup of Sales.
How should you complete the Transact-SQL statement? To answer, select the appropriate options in the answer area.
NOTE: Each correct selection is worth one point.
A. Mastered

B. Not Mastered
Answer: A

QUESTION: 123
-
You have an Azure SQL database named DB 1 in the General Purpose service tier. You need to monitor DB 1 by using SQL Insights.
What should you include in the solution? To answer, select the appropriate options in the answer area. NOTE: Each correct selection is worth one point.
A. Mastered
B. Not Mastered
Answer: A

QUESTION: 124
-
You have an Azure SQL database.
You discover that the plan cache is full of compiled plans that were used only once.
You run the select * from sys.database_scoped_configurations Transact-SQL command and receive the results shown in the following table.
You need relieve the memory pressure. What should you configure?
A. LEGACY_CARDINALITY_ESTIMATION
B. QUERY_OPTIMIZER_HOTFIXES
C. OPTIMIZE_FOR_AD_HOC_WORKLOADS
D. ACCELERATED_PLAN_FORCING
Answer: C

QUESTION: 125
-
You have a 50-TB Microsoft SQL Server database named DB1.
You need to reduce the time it takes to perform database consistency checks of DB1.
Which Transact-SQL command should you run? To answer, select the appropriate options in the answer area.
NOTE: Each correct selection is worth one point.
A. Mastered
B. Not Mastered
Answer: A

QUESTION: 126
-
You have an Azure Databricks workspace named workspace1 in the Standard pricing tier. Workspace1 contains an all-purpose cluster named cluster1.
You need to reduce the time it takes for cluster1 to start and scale up. The solution must minimize costs. What should you do first?
A. Upgrade workspace1 to the Premium pricing tier.
B. Configure a global init script for workspace1.
C. Create a pool in workspace1.

D. Create a cluster policy in workspace1.
Answer: C

QUESTION: 127

-

You have an Azure SQL managed instance.
You need to restore a database named DB1 by using Transact-SQL.
Which command should you run? To answer, select the appropriate options in the answer area.
NOTE: Each correct selection is worth one point.

A. Mastered
B. Not Mastered
Answer: A

QUESTION: 128

-

You have an Azure subscription that is linked to an Azure AD tenant named contoso.com. The subscription contains an Azure SQL database named SQL 1 and an
Azure web named app1. App1 has the managed identity feature enabled. You need to create a new database user for app1.
How should you complete the Transact-SQL statement? To answer, select the appropriate options in the answer area.
NOTE: Each correct selection is worth one point.
A. Mastered
B. Not Mastered
Answer: A
Explanation:
https://learn.microsoft.com/en-us/azure/app-service/tutorial-connect-msi-sql-database?tabs=windowsclient%2Ce

QUESTION: 129

-

You have the following Transact-SQL query.
Which column returned by the query represents the free space in each file?
A. ColumnA
B. ColumnB
C. ColumnC
D. ColumnD
Answer: C

QUESTION: 130

-

You are building an Azure virtual machine.

You allocate two 1-TiB, P30 premium storage disks to the virtual machine. Each disk provides 5,000 IOPS. You plan to migrate an on-premises instance of
Microsoft SQL Server to the virtual machine. The instance has a database that contains a 1.2-TiB data file. The database requires 10,000 IOPS.
You need to configure storage for the virtual machine to support the database.
Which three objects should you create in sequence? To answer, move the appropriate objects from the list of objects to the answer area and arrange them in the
correct order.
A. Mastered
B. Not Mastered
Answer: A

QUESTION: 131

-

You have two on-premises Microsoft SQL Server 2019 instances named SQL1 and SQL2.
You need to migrate the databases hosted on SQL 1 to Azure. The solution must meet the following requirements:
The service that hosts the migrated databases must be able to communicate with SQL2 by using linked server connections.
Administrative effort must be minimized. What should you use to host the databases?
A. a single Azure SQL database
B. an Azure SQL Database elastic pool
C. SQL Server on Azure Virtual Machines
D. Azure SQL Managed Instance
Answer: D

QUESTION: 132

-

You have SQL Server on Azure virtual machines in an availability group. You have a database named DB1 that is NOT in the availability group.
You create a full database backup of DB1. You need to add DB1 to the availability group.
Which restore option should you use on the secondary replica?
A. Restore with Recovery
B. Restore with Norecovery
C. Restore with Standby
Answer: B

QUESTION: 133

-

You have an Azure virtual machine based on a custom image named VM1. VM1 hosts an instance of Microsoft SQL Server 2019 Standard.
You need to automate the maintenance of VM1 to meet the following requirements: Automate the patching of SQL Server and Windows Server.
Automate full database backups and transaction log backups of the databases on VM1.
Minimize administrative effort. What should you do first?
A. Enable a system-assigned managed identity for VM1

B. Register VM1 to the Microsoft.Sql resource provider
C. Install an Azure virtual machine Desired State Configuration (DSC) extension on VM1
D. Register VM1 to the Microsoft.SqlVirtualMachine resource provider
Answer: B

QUESTION: 134

-

You are developing an application that uses Azure Data Lake Storage Gen 2.
You need to recommend a solution to grant permissions to a specific application for a limited time period. What should you include in the recommendation?
A. role assignments
B. account keys
C. shared access signatures (SAS)
D. Azure Active Directory (Azure AD) identities
Answer: C

QUESTION: 135

-

Note: This question is part of a series of questions that present the same scenario. Each question in the series contains a unique solution that might meet the
stated goals. Some question sets might have more than one correct solution, while others might not have a correct solution.
After you answer a question in this section, you will NOT be able to return to it. As a result, these questions will not appear in the review screen.
You have two Azure SQL Database servers named Server1 and Server2. Each server contains an Azure SQL database named Database1.
You need to restore Database1 from Server1 to Server2. The solution must replace the existing Database1 on Server2.
Solution: You restore Database1 from Server1 to the Server2 by using the RESTORE Transact-SQL command and the REPLACE option.
Does this meet the goal?
A. Yes
B. No
Answer: A

QUESTION: 136

-

You have an Azure subscription.
You plan to deploy an Azure SQL database by using an Azure Resource Manager template.
How should you complete the template? To answer, select the appropriate options in the answer area.
NOTE: Each correct selection is worth one point.
A. Mastered
B. Not Mastered
Answer: A
Explanation:

Text Description automatically generated
Reference:
https://docs.microsoft.com/en-us/azure/azure-sql/database/single-database-create-arm-template-quickstart

QUESTION: 137

-

You have an Azure SQL database named sqldb1.
You need to minimize the possibility of Query Store transitioning to a read-only state. What should you do?
A. Double the value of Data Flush interval
B. Decrease by half the value of Data Flush Interval
C. Double the value of Statistics Collection Interval
D. Decrease by half the value of Statistics Collection interval
Answer: B

QUESTION: 138

-

You have four Azure subscriptions. Each subscription contains multiple Azure SQL databases. You need to update the column and index statistics for the databases.
What should you use?
A. an Azure Automation runbook
B. a SQL Agent job
C. Azure SQL Analytics
D. automatic tuning in Azure SQL Database
Answer: A

QUESTION: 139

-

A data engineer creates a table to store employee information for a new application. All employee names are in the US English alphabet. All addresses are locations in the United States. The data engineer uses the following statement to create the table.
You need to recommend changes to the data types to reduce storage and improve performance. Which two actions should you recommend? Each correct answer presents part of the solution. NOTE: Each correct selection is worth one point.
A. Change Salary to the money data type.
B. Change PhoneNumber to the float data type.
C. Change LastHireDate to the datetime2(7) data type.
D. Change PhoneNumber to the bigint data type.
E. Change LastHireDate to the date data type.
Answer: AE

QUESTION: 140

-

Note: This question is part of a series of questions that present the same scenario. Each question in the series contains a unique solution that might meet the stated goals. Some question sets might have more than one correct solution, while others might not have a correct solution.
After you answer a question in this section, you will NOT be able to return to it. As a result, these questions will not appear in the review screen.
You have an Azure Data Lake Storage account that contains a staging zone.
You need to design a daily process to ingest incremental data from the staging zone, transform the data by executing an R script, and then insert the transformed data into a data warehouse in Azure Synapse Analytics.
Solution: You use an Azure Data Factory schedule trigger to execute a pipeline that executes mapping data flow, and then inserts the data into the data warehouse.
Does this meet the goal?
A. Yes
B. No
Answer: B

QUESTION: 141

-

You have an Azure SQL database named db1 on a server named server1. You need to modify the MAXDOP settings for db1.
What should you do?
A. Connect to db1 and run the sp_configure command.
B. Connect to the master database of server1 and run the sp_configure command.
C. Configure the extended properties of db1.
D. Modify the database scoped configuration of db1.
Answer: D

QUESTION: 142

-

You have the following Azure Resource Manager template.
For each of the following statements, select Yes if the statement is true. Otherwise, select No.
NOTE: Each correct selection is worth one point.
A. Mastered
B. Not Mastered
Answer: A

QUESTION: 143

-

You have an Azure SQL database named DB1. DB1 contains a table that has a column named Col1. You need to encrypt the data in Col1.

Which four actions should you perform for DB1 in sequence? To answer, move the appropriate actions from the list of actions to the answer area and arrange
them in the correct order.

A. Mastered
B. Not Mastered
Answer: A

QUESTION: 144

-

You have a SQL pool in Azure Synapse that contains a table named dbo.Customers. The table contains a column name Email.
You need to prevent nonadministrative users from seeing the full email addresses in the Email column. The users must see values in a format of
aXXX@XXXX.com instead.
What should you do?
A. From the Azure portal, set a mask on the Email column.
B. From the Azure portal, set a sensitivity classification of Confidential for the Email column.
C. From Microsoft SQL Server Management Studio, set an email mask on the Email column.
D. From Microsoft SQL Server Management Studio, grant the SELECT permission to the users for all the columns in the dbo.Customers table except Email.
Answer: B

QUESTION: 145

-

You have SQL Server 2019 on an Azure virtual machine that contains an SSISDB database. A recent failure causes the master database to be lost.
You discover that all Microsoft SQL Server integration Services (SSIS) packages fail to run on the virtual machine.
Which four actions should you perform in sequence to resolve the issue? To answer, move the appropriate actions from the list of actions to the answer area and
arrange them in the correct.
A. Mastered
B. Not Mastered
Answer: A

QUESTION: 146

-

Note: This question is part of a series of questions that present the same scenario. Each question in the series contains a unique solution that might meet the
stated goals. Some question sets might have more than one correct solution, while others might not have a correct solution.
After you answer a question in this section, you will NOT be able to return to it. As a result, these questions will not appear in the review screen.

You have an Azure Synapse Analytics dedicated SQL pool that contains a table named Table1. You have files that are ingested and loaded into an Azure Data
Lake Storage Gen2 container named
container1.
You plan to insert data from the files into Table1 and transform the data. Each row of data in the files will produce one row in the serving layer of Table1.
You need to ensure that when the source data files are loaded to container1, the DateTime is stored as an additional column in Table1.
Solution: You use an Azure Synapse Analytics serverless SQL pool to create an external table that has an additional DateTime column.
Does this meet the goal?
A. Yes
B. No
Answer: A

QUESTION: 147

-

You need to trigger an Azure Data Factory pipeline when a file arrives in an Azure Data Lake Storage Gen2 container.
Which resource provider should you enable?
A. Microsoft.EventHub
B. Microsoft.EventGrid
C. Microsoft.Sql
D. Microsoft.Automation
Answer: B

QUESTION: 148

-

You have an on-premises Microsoft SQL Server 2016 server named Server1 that contains a database named DB1.
You need to perform an online migration of DB1 to an Azure SQL Database managed instance by using Azure Database Migration Service.
How should you configure the backup of DB1? To answer, select the appropriate options in the answer area. NOTE: Each correct selection is worth one point.
A. Mastered
B. Not Mastered
Answer: A

QUESTION: 149

-

You manage 100 Azure SQL managed instances located across 10 Azure regions.
You need to receive voice message notifications when a maintenance event affects any of the 10 regions. The solution must minimize administrative effort.
What should you do?
A. From the Azure portal, create a service health alert.
B. From the Azure portal, create an Azure Advisor operational excellence alert.

C. From Microsoft SQL Server Management Studio (SSMS), configure a SQL Server agent job.
D. From the Azure portal, configure an activity log alert.
Answer: C

QUESTION: 150

-

You have an Azure Data Factory instance named ADF1 and two Azure Synapse Analytics workspaces named WS1 and WS2.
ADF1 contains the following pipelines:
P1:Uses a copy activity to copy data from a nonpartitioned table in a dedicated SQL pool of WS1 to an Azure Data Lake Storage Gen2 account
P2:Uses a copy activity to copy data from text-delimited files in an Azure Data Lake Storage Gen2 account to a nonpartitioned table in a dedicated SQL pool of
WS2
You need to configure P1 and P2 to maximize parallelism and performance.
Which dataset settings should you configure for the copy activity of each pipeline? To answer, select the appropriate options in the answer area.
A. Mastered
B. Not Mastered
Answer: A

QUESTION: 151

-

You are designing an enterprise data warehouse in Azure Synapse Analytics that will store website traffic analytics in a star schema.
You plan to have a fact table for website visits. The table will be approximately 5 GB.
You need to recommend which distribution type and index type to use for the table. The solution must provide the fastest query performance.
What should you recommend? To answer, select the appropriate options in the answer area.
NOTE: Each correct selection is worth one point.
A. Mastered
B. Not Mastered
Answer: A

QUESTION: 152

-

You plan to develop a dataset named Purchases by using Azure Databricks. Purchases will contain the following columns:
ProductID
ItemPrice
LineTotal
Quantity
StoreID
Minute
Month
Hour

Year
Day
You need to store the data to support hourly incremental load pipelines that will vary for each StoreID. The solution must minimize storage costs.
How should you complete the code? To answer, select the appropriate options in the answer area.
NOTE: Each correct selection is worth one point.
A. Mastered
B. Not Mastered
Answer: A

QUESTION: 153

-

You are designing an enterprise data warehouse in Azure Synapse Analytics that will contain a table named Customers. Customers will contain credit card
information.
You need to recommend a solution to provide salespeople with the ability to view all the entries in Customers. The solution must prevent all the salespeople from
viewing or inferring the credit card information.
What should you include in the recommendation?
A. row-level security
B. data masking
C. Always Encrypted
D. column-level security
Answer: B

QUESTION: 154

-

You have SQL Server on an Azure virtual machine.
You need to use Policy-Based Management in Microsoft SQL Server to identify stored procedures that do not comply with your naming conventions.
Which three actions should you perform in sequence? To answer, move the appropriate actions from the list of actions to the answer area and arrange them in the
correct order.

A. Mastered
B. Not Mastered
Answer: A

QUESTION: 155

-

You have SQL Server on an Azure virtual machine that contains a database named DB1. DB1 is 30 TB and has a 1-GB daily rate of change.
You back up the database by using a Microsoft SQL Server Agent job that runs Transact-SQL commands. You perform a weekly full backup on Sunday, daily

differential backups at 01:00, and transaction log backups every five minutes.
The database fails on Wednesday at 10:00.
Which three backups should you restore in sequence? To answer, move the appropriate backups from the list of backups to the answer area and arrange them in
the correct order.
A. Mastered
B. Not Mastered
Answer: A

QUESTION: 156

-

You have an Azure SQL database.
You are reviewing a slow performing query as shown in the following exhibit.
Use the drop-down menus to select the answer choice that completes each statement based on the information presented in the graphic.
NOTE: Each correct selection is worth one point.
A. Mastered
B. Not Mastered
Answer: A

QUESTION: 157

-

You are designing a streaming data solution that will ingest variable volumes of data. You need to ensure that you can change the partition count after creation.
Which service should you use to ingest the data?

A. Azure Event Hubs Standard
B. Azure Stream Analytics
C. Azure Data Factory
D. Azure Event Hubs Dedicated
Answer: D

QUESTION: 158

-

You are planning disaster recovery for the failover group of an Azure SQL Database managed instance.
Your company's SLA requires that the database in the failover group become available as quickly as possible if a major outage occurs.
You set the Read/Write failover policy to Automatic.
What are two results of the configuration? Each correct answer presents a complete solution.
NOTE: Each correct selection is worth one point.
A. In the event of a datacenter or Azure regional outage, the databases will fail over automatically.
B. In the event of an outage, the databases in the primary instance will fail over immediately.
C. In the event of an outage, you can selectively fail over individual databases.

D. In the event of an outage, you can set a different grace period to fail over each database.
E. In the event of an outage, the minimum delay for the databases to fail over in the primary instance will be one hour.
Answer: AE

QUESTION: 159

-

Note: This question is part of a series of questions that present the same scenario. Each question in the series contains a unique solution that might meet the
stated goals. Some question sets might have more than one correct solution, while others might not have a correct solution.
After you answer a question in this section, you will NOT be able to return to it. As a result, these questions will not appear in the review screen.
You have two Azure SQL Database servers named Server1 and Server2. Each server contains an Azure SQL database named Database1.
You need to restore Database1 from Server1 to Server2. The solution must replace the existing Database1 on Server2.
Solution: You run the Remove-AzSqlDatabase PowerShell cmdlet for Database1 on Server2. You run the Restore-AzSqlDatabase PowerShell cmdlet for
Database1 on Server2.
Does this meet the goal?
A. Yes
B. No
Answer: B

QUESTION: 160

-

You have an Azure SQL database.
Users report that the executions of a stored procedure are slower than usual. You suspect that a regressed query is causing the performance issue.
You need to view the query execution plan to verify whether a regressed query is causing the issue. The solution must minimize effort.
What should you use?
A. Performance Recommendations in the Azure portal
B. Extended Events in Microsoft SQL Server Management Studio (SSMS)
C. Query Store in Microsoft SQL Server Management Studio (SSMS)
D. Query Performance Insight in the Azure portal
Answer: C

QUESTION: 161

-

You have an on-premises Microsoft SQL Server 2019 server that hosts a database named DB1.
You have an Azure subscription that contains an Azure SQL managed instance named SQLMI1 and a virtual network named VNET1. SQLMI1 resides on VNET1.
The on-premises network connects to VNET1 by using an ExpressRoute connection.

You plan to migrate DB1 to SQLMI1 by using Azure Database Migration Service. You need to configure VNET1 to support the migration.
What should you do?
A. Configure service endpoints.
B. Configure virtual network peering.
C. Deploy an Azure firewall.
D. Configure network security groups (NSGs).
Answer: A

QUESTION: 162

-

You are monitoring an Azure Stream Analytics job.
You discover that the Backlogged input Events metric is increasing slowly and is consistently non-zero.
You need to ensure that the job can handle all the events. What should you do?
A. Remove any named consumer groups from the connection and use $default.
B. Change the compatibility level of the Stream Analytics job.
C. Create an additional output stream for the existing input stream.
D. Increase the number of streaming units (SUs).
Answer: D

QUESTION: 163

-

You manage an enterprise data warehouse in Azure Synapse Analytics.
Users report slow performance when they run commonly used queries. Users do not report performance changes for infrequently used queries.
You need to monitor resource utilization to determine the source of the performance issues. Which metric should you monitor?
A. Local tempdb percentage
B. DWU percentage
C. Data Warehouse Units (DWU) used
D. Cache hit percentage
Answer: A

QUESTION: 164

-

You are performing exploratory analysis of bus fare data in an Azure Data Lake Storage Gen2 account by using an Azure Synapse Analytics serverless SQL pool.
You execute the Transact-SQL query shown in the following exhibit.
Use the drop-down menus to select the answer choice that completes each statement based on the information presented in the graphic.
A. Mastered
B. Not Mastered
Answer: A

QUESTION: 165

-

You have an Azure Data Factory that contains 10 pipelines.
You need to label each pipeline with its main purpose of either ingest, transform, or load. The labels must be available for grouping and filtering when using the monitoring experience in Data Factory.
What should you add to each pipeline?
A. an annotation
B. a resource tag
C. a run group ID
D. a user property
E. a correlation ID
Answer: A

QUESTION: 166

-

You have a version-8.0 Azure Database for MySQL database.
You need to identify which database queries consume the most resources. Which tool should you use?
A. Query Store
B. Metrics
C. Query Performance Insight
D. Alerts
Answer: A

QUESTION: 167

-

You have the following Azure Data Factory pipelines:
Ingest Data from System1
Ingest Data from System2
Populate Dimensions
Populate Facts
Ingest Data from System1 and Ingest Data from System2 have no dependencies. Populate Dimensions must execute after Ingest Data from System1 and Ingest Data from System2. Populate Facts must execute after the Populate Dimensions pipeline. All the pipelines must execute every eight hours.
What should you do to schedule the pipelines for execution?
A. Add a schedule trigger to all four pipelines.
B. Add an event trigger to all four pipelines.
C. Create a parent pipeline that contains the four pipelines and use an event trigger.
D. Create a parent pipeline that contains the four pipelines and use a schedule trigger.
Answer: D

QUESTION:168

-

You have an Azure subscription that contains an Azure SQL database named SQL1. SQL1 is in an Azure region that does not support availability zones.

You need to ensure that you have a secondary replica of SQLI in the same region. What should you use?
A. log shipping
B. auto-failover groups
C. active geo-replication
D. Microsoft SQL Server failover clusters
Answer: C

QUESTION: 169

-

You have SQL Server on an Azure virtual machine named SQL1. SQL1 has an agent job to back up all databases.
You add a user named dbadmin1 as a SQL Server Agent operator. You need to ensure that dbadmin1 receives an email alert if a job fails.
Which three actions should you perform in sequence? To answer, move the appropriate actions from the list of actions to the answer area and arrange them in the
correct order.
A. Mastered
B. Not Mastered
Answer: A

QUESTION: 170

-

Your on-premises network contains a Microsoft SQL Server 2016 server that hosts a database named db1. You have an Azure subscription.
You plan to migrate db1 to an Azure SQL managed instance.
You need to create the SQL managed instance. The solution must minimize the disk latency of the instance. Which service tier should you use?
A. Hyperscale
B. General Purpose
C. Premium
D. Business Critical
Answer: A

QUESTION: 171

-

You have an Azure subscription that contains the resources shown in the following table.
You need to back up db1 to mysqlbackups, and then restore the backup to a new database named db2 that is hosted on SQL1. The solution must ensure that db1
is backed up to a stripe set.
Which three Transact-SQL statements should you execute in sequence? To answer, move the appropriate statements from the list of statements to the answer
area and arrange them in the correct order.
A. Mastered
B. Not Mastered
Answer: A

QUESTION: 172

-

You plan to move two 100-GB databases to Azure.
You need to dynamically scale resources consumption based on workloads. The solution must minimize downtime during scaling operations.
What should you use?

A. two Azure SQL Databases in an elastic pool
B. two databases hosted in SQL Server on an Azure virtual machine
C. two databases in an Azure SQL Managed instance
D. two single Azure SQL databases

Answer: D

QUESTION: 173

-

You create five Azure SQL Database instances on the same logical server.
In each database, you create a user for an Azure Active Directory (Azure AD) user named User1.
User1 attempts to connect to the logical server by using Azure
Data Studio and receives a login error.
You need to ensure that when User1 connects to the logical server by using Azure Data Studio, User1 can see all the databases.
What should you do?

A. Create User1 in the master database.
B. Assign User1 the db_datareader role for the master database.
C. Assign User1 the db_datareader role for the databases that Userl creates.
D. Grant select on sys.databases to public in the master database.

Answer: A

QUESTION: 174

-

You have an Azure SQL database that contains a table named Employees. Employees contains a column named Salary.
You need to encrypt the Salary column. The solution must prevent database administrators from reading the data in the Salary column and must provide the most
secure encryption.
Which three actions should you perform in sequence? To answer, move the appropriate actions from the list of actions to the answer area and arrange them in the
correct order.

A. Mastered
B. Not Mastered

Answer: A

QUESTION: 175

-

You are building an Azure Stream Analytics job to retrieve game data.

You need to ensure that the job returns the highest scoring record for each five-minute time interval of each game.
How should you complete the Stream Analytics query? To answer, select the appropriate options in the answer area.
NOTE: Each correct selection is worth one point.
A. Mastered
B. Not Mastered
Answer: A

QUESTION: 176
-
You have an Azure SQL database named DB1.
You need to ensure that DB1 will support automatic failover without data loss if a datacenter fails. The solution must minimize costs.
Which deployment option and pricing tier should you configure?

A. Azure SQL Database Premium
B. Azure SQL Database serverless
C. Azure SQL Database managed instance Business Critical
D. Azure SQL Database Standard
Answer: A

QUESTION: 177
-
You have an Azure subscription.
You plan to deploy a new Azure virtual machine that will host a Microsoft SQL Server instance.
You need to configure the disks on the virtual machine. The solution must meet the following requirements:
• Minimize latency for transaction logs.
• Minimize the impact on IO Of the virtual machine.
Which type of disk should you use for each workload? To answer. drag the appropriate disk types to the correct workloads. Each disk type may be used once, at
all. You may need to drag the split bar between panes or scroll to view content.
NOTE: Each correct selection is worth one point.
A. Mastered
B. Not Mastered
Answer: A

QUESTION: 178
-
You have an Azure Data Factory pipeline that performs an incremental load of source data to an Azure Data Lake Storage Gen2 account.
Data to be loaded is identified by a column named LastUpdatedDate in the source table. You plan to execute the pipeline every four hours.

You need to ensure that the pipeline execution meets the following requirements:
Automatically retries the execution when the pipeline run fails due to concurrency or throttling limits. Supports backfilling existing data in the table.
Which type of trigger should you use?
A. tumbling window
B. on-demand
C. event
D. schedule
Answer: A

QUESTION: 179

-

You have an Azure SQL database named db1 on a server named server1. You use Query Performance Insight to monitor db1.
You need to modify the Query Store configuration to ensure that performance monitoring data is available as soon as possible.
Which configuration setting should you modify and which value should you configure? To answer, select the appropriate options in the answer area.
NOTE: Each correct selection is worth one point.
A. Mastered
B. Not Mastered
Answer: A

QUESTION: 180

-

You have an Azure SQL managed instance named SQLMI1 that has Resource Governor enabled and is used by two apps named App1 and App2.
You need to configure SQLMI1 to limit the CPU and memory resources that can be allocated to App1. Which four actions should you perform in sequence? To
answer, move the appropriate actions from the list of actions to the answer area and arrange them in the correct order.
A. Mastered
B. Not Mastered
Answer: A

QUESTION: 181

-

Note: This question is part of a series of questions that present the same scenario. Each question in the series contains a unique solution that might meet the
stated goals. Some question sets might have more than one correct solution, while others might not have a correct solution.
After you answer a question in this section, you will NOT be able to return to it. As a result, these questions will not appear in the review screen.
You have two Azure SQL Database servers named Server1 and Server2. Each server contains an Azure SQL database named Database1.

You need to restore Database1 from Server1 to Server2. The solution must replace the existing Database1 on Server2.
Solution: From Microsoft SQL Server Management Studio (SSMS), you rename Database1 on Server2 as Database2. From the Azure portal, you create a new
database on Server2 by restoring the backup of Database1 from Server1, and then you delete Database2.
Does this meet the goal?
A. Yes
B. No

Answer: B

QUESTION: 182
-
You have an Azure subscription that contains the resources shown in the following table.
App1 experiences transient connection errors and timeouts when it attempts to access db1 after extended periods of inactivity. You need to modify db1 to resolve
the issues experienced by App1 as soon as possible, without considering immediate costs. What should you do?
A. Increase the number Of vCores allocated to db1.
B. Disable auto-pause delay for dbl.
C. Decrease the auto-pause delay for db1.
D. Enable automatic tuning for db1.
Answer: D

QUESTION: 183
-
You have an Azure data factory that has two pipelines named PipelineA and PipelineB. PipelineA has four activities as shown in the following exhibit.
PipelineB has two activities as shown in the following exhibit.
You create an alert for the data factory that uses Failed pipeline runs metrics for both pipelines and all failure types. The metric has the following settings:
Operator: Greater than
Aggregation type: Total
Threshold value: 2
Aggregation granularity (Period): 5 minutes
Frequency of evaluation: Every 5 minutes
Data Factory monitoring records the failures shown in the following table.
For each of the following statements, select Yes if the statement is true. Otherwise, select No.
NOTE: Each correct selection is worth one point.
A. Mastered
B. Not Mastered
Answer: A

QUESTION: 184

-

You receive numerous alerts from Azure Monitor for an Azure SQL database.

You need to reduce the number of alerts. You must only receive alerts if there is a significant change in usage patterns for an extended period.

Which two actions should you perform? Each correct answer presents part of the solution. NOTE: Each correct selection is worth one point.

A. Set Threshold Sensitivity to High

B. Set the Alert logic threshold to Dynamic

C. Set the Alert logic threshold to Static

D. Set Threshold Sensitivity to Low

E. Set Force Plan to On

Answer: BD

QUESTION: 185

-

You have two Azure virtual machines named VM1 and VM2 that run Windows Server 2019. VM1 and VM2 each host a default Microsoft SQL Server 2019

instance. VM1 contains a database named DB1 that is backed up to a file named D:\DB1.bak.

You plan to deploy an Always On availability group that will have the following configurations:

VM1 will host the primary replica of DB1.

VM2 will host a secondary replica of DB1.

You need to prepare the secondary database on VM2 for the availability group.

How should you complete the Transact-SQL statement? To answer, select the appropriate options in the answer area.

A. Mastered

B. Not Mastered

Answer: A

QUESTION: 186

-

You have a data warehouse in Azure Synapse Analytics.

You need to ensure that the data in the data warehouse is encrypted at rest. What should you enable?

A. Transparent Data Encryption (TDE)

B. Advanced Data Security for this database

C. Always Encrypted for all columns

D. Secure transfer required

Answer: A

QUESTION: 187

-

You have an Azure virtual machine named VM1 on a virtual network named VNet1. Outbound traffic from VM1 to the internet is blocked.

You have an Azure SQL database named SqlDb1 on a logical server named SqlSrv1.

You need to implement connectivity between VM1 and SqlDb1 to meet the following requirements:

Ensure that all traffic to the public endpoint of SqlSrv1 is blocked.
Minimize the possibility of VM1 exfiltrating data stored in SqlDb1. What should you create on VNet1?
A. a VPN gateway
B. a service endpoint
C. a private link
D. an ExpressRoute gateway
Answer: C
QUESTION: 188
-
You have an Azure SQL database named DB3.
You need to provide a user named DevUser with the ability to view the properties of DB3 from Microsoft SQL Server Management Studio (SSMS) as shown in the
exhibit. (Click the Exhibit tab.)
Which Transact-SQL command should you run?
A. GRANT SHOWPLAN TO DevUser
B. GRANT VIEW DEFINITION TO DevUser
C. GRANT VIEW DATABASE STATE TO DevUser
D. GRANT SELECT TO DevUser
Answer: C

QUESTION: 189
-
You have an Azure SQL database named DB1.
You need to display the estimated execution plan of a query by using the query editor in the Azure portal. What should you do first?
A. Run the set showplan_all Transact-SQL statement.
B. For DB1, set QUERY_CAPTURE_MODE of Query Store to All.
C. Run the set forceplan Transact-SQL statement.
D. Enable Query Store for DB1.
Answer: A

QUESTION: 190
-
You need to apply 20 built-in Azure Policy definitions to all new and existing Azure SQL Database deployments in an Azure subscription. The solution must
minimize administrative effort.
Which three actions should you perform in sequence? To answer, move the appropriate actions from the list of actions to the answer area and arrange them in the
correct order.
A. Mastered
B. Not Mastered
Answer: A

QUESTION: 191
-

You have an Azure Synapse Analytics workspace named WS1 that contains an Apache Spark pool named Pool1.
You plan to create a database named DB1 in Pool1.
You need to ensure that when tables are created in DB1, the tables are available automatically as external tables to the built-in serverless SQL pool.
Which format should you use for the tables in DB1?
A. JSON
B. CSV
C. Parquet
D. ORC
Answer: C

QUESTION: 192

-
You have an Azure virtual machine named VM1 on a virtual network named VNet1. Outbound traffic from VM1 to the internet is blocked.
You have an Azure SQL database named SqlDb1 on a logical server named SqlSrv1.
You need to implement connectivity between VM1 and SqlDb1 to meet the following requirements:
Ensure that VM1 cannot connect to any Azure SQL Server other than SqlSrv1.
Restrict network connectivity to SqlSrv1. What should you create on VNet1?
A. a VPN gateway
B. a service endpoint
C. a private link
D. an ExpressRoute gateway
Answer: B

QUESTION: 193

-
You are designing a security model for an Azure Synapse Analytics dedicated SQL pool that will support multiple companies.
You need to ensure that users from each company can view only the data of their respective company. Which two objects should you include in the solution? Each
correct answer presents part of the solution. NOTE: Each correct selection is worth one point.
A. a column encryption key
B. asymmetric keys
C. a function
D. a custom role-based access control (RBAC) role
E. a security policy
Answer: DE

ONLINE RESOURCES

Practice Paper

Link : https://forms.gle/GKXFurkEVr9MyNBU8

QR Code :

Video Content

Link : https://www.youtube.com/playlist?list=PLzlh_31VWEFpv-rmc2mbpoIqUOqVW_cIo

QR Code :

Chapter 3: Viva Voce Questions

Q 1: What is the role of an Azure Database Administrator?
Answer: An Azure Database Administrator is responsible for managing, monitoring, and optimizing data solutions in Azure, including SQL Server and other database technologies hosted in Azure environments.
Q 2: What are Azure SQL Database and Azure SQL Managed Instance?
Answer: Azure SQL Database is a fully managed platform as a service (PaaS) database engine that handles most database management functions. Azure SQL Managed Instance offers near 100% compatibility with the latest SQL Server on-premises features.
Q 3: How does Azure ensure database security?
Answer: Azure provides multiple layers of security including network security, access management, threat protection, and information protection using tools like Azure Active Directory, firewalls, and encryption.
Q 4: Can you explain the Azure SQL Database's backup and recovery features?
Answer: Azure SQL Database automatically creates and stores backups, supports point-in-time restores, and facilitates geo-replication for disaster recovery scenarios.
Q 5: What is the purpose of the Azure Data Factory?
Answer: Azure Data Factory is a data integration service that allows you to create data-driven workflows for orchestrating and automating data movement and data transformation.
Q 6: Describe the process of performance tuning in Azure SQL Database.
Answer: Performance tuning in Azure SQL involves monitoring and optimizing database performance through query tuning, indexing, resource allocation, and using performance insights provided by Azure.
Q 7: What are Elastic Pools in Azure SQL Database?
Answer: Elastic Pools are a cost-effective solution to manage and scale multiple databases that have variable and unpredictable usage demands, sharing resources within a single pool.
Q 8: How does Azure Monitor aid database administrators?
Answer: Azure Monitor collects, analyzes, and acts on telemetry data from Azure and on-premises environments, helping administrators track health, performance, and other important metrics.
Q 9: What are some common replication strategies in Azure SQL Database?
Answer: Common replication strategies include using Active Geo-Replication for real-time replication and failover, as well as auto-failover groups for managing replication and failover at a group level.
Q 10: Explain the role of Azure Advisor in database management.
Answer: Azure Advisor provides personalized recommendations to optimize database performance, enhance security, and reduce costs by analyzing your deployed services and usage patterns.
Q 11: How do you manage data migration to Azure SQL Database?
Answer: Data migration to Azure SQL Database can be managed using tools like the Azure Database Migration Service, which simplifies the process of migrating from various database systems to Azure.
Q 12: What is Database Sharding in Azure?
Answer: Database sharding involves distributing data across multiple databases or shards to improve scalability, performance, and manageability in large database applications.
Q 13: Describe the importance of indexing in Azure SQL Database.

Answer: Indexing is crucial for improving query performance and speed by allowing the SQL Server engine to quickly locate and retrieve data without scanning the entire table.

Q 14: What is the difference between DTU-based and vCore-based purchasing models in Azure SQL Database?

Answer: DTU (Database Throughput Unit)-based model offers a blend of compute, memory, and IO resources in a single bundle, whereas vCore-based model provides more flexibility and control over individual compute, memory, and storage settings.

Q 15: How does Azure handle database scaling?

Answer: Azure handles database scaling through vertical scaling (adjusting resources per instance) and horizontal scaling (adding more instances), depending on the demand and configuration.

Q 16: What is Partitioning in Azure SQL Database?

Answer: Partitioning in Azure SQL Database involves dividing large tables and indexes into smaller, more manageable pieces, improving performance and management of large datasets.

Q 17: How do you implement High Availability (HA) in Azure SQL Database?

Answer: High Availability can be implemented using failover groups, availability zones, and auto-failover groups that ensure database continuity and minimal downtime.

Q 18: What are Azure SQL Analytics?

Answer: Azure SQL Analytics is an advanced monitoring solution that provides an in-depth view of SQL database performance metrics, enabling proactive management and tuning.

Q 19: Explain how Azure uses machine learning for database management.

Answer: Azure uses machine learning for features like automatic tuning, which predicts and automatically adjusts performance settings to improve efficiency and reduce workload management overhead.

Q 20: How does Azure ensure compliance and regulatory adherence for databases?

Answer: Azure ensures compliance through a comprehensive set of compliance offerings, regular audits, certifications, data protection standards, and built-in controls to meet regulatory requirements.

Q1. Which Azure SQL deployment option provides the highest compatibility with on-premises SQL Server?

A. Azure SQL Database
B. Azure SQL Managed Instance
C. Azure Cosmos DB
D. Azure Table Storage

Answer: B. Azure SQL Managed Instance
Reasoning:
Azure SQL Managed Instance provides the highest compatibility with on-premises SQL Server because it supports instance-level features such as SQL Agent, cross-database queries, linked servers, Service Broker, and near-full SQL Server surface area. Azure SQL Database is a PaaS database-level service and does not support every instance-level feature. Managed Instance is commonly selected for lift-and-shift migrations where applications depend on SQL Server features that are not available in single database or elastic pool models.

Q2. Which Azure SQL option is best for a single modern application database with minimal administration?

A. Azure SQL Database single database
B. SQL Server on Azure VM
C. Azure SQL Managed Instance
D. Azure Storage Table

Answer: A. Azure SQL Database single database
Reasoning:
Azure SQL Database single database is ideal when an application needs one isolated database with built-in backups, patching, high availability, and scaling. It is a fully managed PaaS service, so Microsoft manages the underlying infrastructure. SQL Server on Azure VM gives more control but requires more administration. Managed Instance is better when instance-level compatibility is required. For modern applications that do not need full SQL Server instance features, a single Azure SQL Database is usually the simplest and most efficient option.

Q3. What is the main benefit of using elastic pools in Azure SQL Database?

A. Encrypting data
B. Sharing resources across multiple databases
C. Replacing backups
D. Creating virtual networks

Answer: B. Sharing resources across multiple databases
Reasoning:
Elastic pools allow multiple Azure SQL databases to share a common set of compute resources. This is useful when databases have unpredictable or varying usage patterns. Instead of

provisioning each database for peak demand, databases use shared resources from the pool. This can reduce cost while maintaining performance. Elastic pools are especially useful for SaaS applications with many customer databases. They do not replace backup, encryption, or networking features; their main purpose is performance and cost management across multiple databases.

Q4. Which purchasing model uses vCores and allows choosing compute and storage independently?

A. DTU model
B. vCore model
C. Serverless only
D. Basic tier only

Answer: B. vCore model
Reasoning:
The vCore purchasing model lets administrators choose compute, memory, and storage more transparently. It is useful when organizations want flexibility and predictable sizing similar to on-premises SQL Server. It also supports Azure Hybrid Benefit for eligible SQL Server licenses. The DTU model combines compute, memory, and I/O into bundled performance units, which is simpler but less flexible. For DP-300, understanding vCore helps with performance planning, cost estimation, scaling, and choosing between General Purpose, Business Critical, and Hyperscale service tiers.

Q5. Which Azure SQL service tier provides the lowest latency by using local SSD storage?

A. Basic
B. General Purpose
C. Business Critical
D. Archive

Answer: C. Business Critical
Reasoning:
The Business Critical tier is designed for high-performance workloads that require low latency and high availability. It uses local SSD storage and multiple replicas, providing faster I/O performance than General Purpose. General Purpose uses remote storage, which is cost-effective but may have higher latency. Business Critical is suitable for mission-critical OLTP workloads with high transaction rates. It also supports readable secondary replicas, making it useful for read scale-out scenarios. The tier costs more but provides stronger performance and availability features.

Q6. What is Azure SQL Hyperscale best suited for?

A. Very small databases only
B. Large databases requiring rapid scale and fast backup
C. Replacing Microsoft Entra ID

D. Managing DNS records

Answer: B. Large databases requiring rapid scale and fast backup
Reasoning:
Azure SQL Database Hyperscale is designed for very large databases and workloads requiring rapid scale-out and fast backup/restore operations. Its architecture separates compute and storage, allowing databases to grow far beyond traditional limits. Backups are storage-snapshot based, making them faster and less intrusive. Hyperscale is suitable for applications with large data volumes and changing performance needs. It is not an identity, DNS, or small-only database solution. DP-300 candidates should know when Hyperscale is a better choice than General Purpose or Business Critical.

Q7. Which tool is commonly used to assess SQL Server migration readiness to Azure?

A. Azure Migrate
B. Azure DNS
C. Azure Bastion
D. Azure Firewall

Answer: A. Azure Migrate
Reasoning:
Azure Migrate helps assess on-premises workloads for migration to Azure, including SQL Server environments. It can discover databases, assess compatibility, estimate sizing, and recommend target Azure SQL options. For database-specific analysis, Data Migration Assistant may also be used, but Azure Migrate is a central migration assessment platform. DNS, Bastion, and Firewall serve networking or security purposes, not migration readiness assessment. In DP-300, migration planning includes identifying blockers, compatibility issues, performance requirements, and the right target platform.

Q8. Which tool can identify compatibility issues before migrating SQL Server databases?

A. Data Migration Assistant
B. Azure Monitor
C. Microsoft Defender for Cloud
D. Azure Key Vault

Answer: A. Data Migration Assistant
Reasoning:
Data Migration Assistant (DMA) helps detect compatibility issues that may block or affect migration from SQL Server to Azure SQL Database, Managed Instance, or newer SQL Server versions. It can identify deprecated features, breaking changes, and unsupported objects. This helps DBAs plan remediation before migration. Azure Monitor collects metrics and logs after deployment, Defender helps with security, and Key Vault stores secrets. DMA is specifically designed for migration assessment and is highly relevant for DP-300 migration planning scenarios.

Q9. Which service supports online database migration with minimal downtime?

A. Azure Database Migration Service
B. Azure Advisor
C. Azure Policy
D. Azure Cost Management

Answer: A. Azure Database Migration Service
Reasoning:
Azure Database Migration Service supports database migrations to Azure with offline and online migration options. Online migration minimizes downtime by continuously replicating changes until cutover. This is important for production databases where long downtime is unacceptable. Azure Advisor gives recommendations, Azure Policy enforces governance, and Cost Management tracks spending. For DP-300, you should understand when to choose offline migration for simpler scenarios and online migration for business-critical workloads requiring minimal interruption.

Q10. Which Azure SQL feature helps protect sensitive data by masking it in query results?

A. Dynamic Data Masking
B. Transparent Data Encryption
C. Automatic tuning
D. Query Store

Answer: A. Dynamic Data Masking
Reasoning:
Dynamic Data Masking limits exposure of sensitive data by masking query results for non-privileged users. For example, email addresses or credit card numbers can be partially hidden. It does not encrypt data at rest; Transparent Data Encryption handles that. It also does not replace permissions, auditing, or Always Encrypted. Dynamic Data Masking is useful as an additional protection layer, especially in applications where users need partial access to data without seeing full sensitive values.

Q11. Which feature encrypts Azure SQL data at rest by default?

A. Transparent Data Encryption
B. Dynamic Data Masking
C. SQL Auditing
D. Query Store

Answer: A. Transparent Data Encryption
Reasoning:
Transparent Data Encryption (TDE) encrypts data files, log files, and backups at rest. Azure SQL Database and Managed Instance use TDE by default to help protect stored data. TDE works transparently without requiring application changes. It protects against offline access to database files or backups, but it does not encrypt data in use or data returned to users. For stronger

protection from administrators or applications, Always Encrypted may be used. DP-300 requires understanding encryption types and when each is appropriate.

Q12. Which feature protects sensitive column data from being visible even to database administrators?

A. Always Encrypted
B. TDE
C. Data masking
D. SQL auditing

Answer: A. Always Encrypted
Reasoning:
Always Encrypted protects sensitive column data by encrypting and decrypting data on the client side. Encryption keys are not exposed to the database engine, so even database administrators cannot view plaintext values. This is useful for highly sensitive information such as national IDs, salaries, or credit card numbers. TDE protects data at rest but DBAs can still query plaintext. Dynamic Data Masking hides output but does not encrypt data. Always Encrypted provides stronger separation between data owners and database administrators.

Q13. What is the purpose of Microsoft Entra authentication for Azure SQL?

A. Manage DNS
B. Authenticate users using centralized cloud identity
C. Replace database backups
D. Increase storage size

Answer: B. Authenticate users using centralized cloud identity
Reasoning:
Microsoft Entra authentication allows Azure SQL users to authenticate with centralized cloud identities rather than SQL logins only. It supports features like Conditional Access, MFA, managed identities, and centralized lifecycle management. This improves security and simplifies administration because identities can be managed in one place. SQL authentication still exists, but Entra authentication is generally preferred for enterprise identity integration. For DP-300, knowing how to configure Entra admins, contained users, and managed identity access is important.

Q14. Which Azure SQL feature records database activities for security and compliance review?

A. Auditing
B. Elastic pool
C. Hyperscale
D. Geo-replication

Answer: A. Auditing
Reasoning:

Azure SQL Auditing tracks database events and writes audit logs to destinations such as Azure Storage, Log Analytics, or Event Hubs. It helps organizations meet compliance requirements and investigate suspicious activity. Auditing can capture events like logins, permission changes, and queries depending on configuration. Elastic pools manage shared performance, Hyperscale handles large database scaling, and geo-replication supports disaster recovery. Auditing is a security and compliance feature that DP-300 administrators must understand and configure properly.

Q15. Which feature provides vulnerability assessment recommendations for Azure SQL?

A. Microsoft Defender for SQL
B. Azure Files
C. Azure DNS
D. Azure Backup vault

Answer: A. Microsoft Defender for SQL
Reasoning:
Microsoft Defender for SQL provides advanced security capabilities, including vulnerability assessment and threat detection. It can identify misconfigurations, excessive permissions, missing security controls, and suspicious database activities. Vulnerability assessment helps DBAs improve security posture by reviewing actionable recommendations. Azure Files, DNS, and Backup vaults are unrelated to SQL vulnerability assessment. In DP-300, security implementation includes auditing, Defender for SQL, authentication, encryption, firewall rules, private endpoints, and least privilege access.

Q16. What is the purpose of Azure SQL firewall rules?

A. Control which IP addresses can access the logical server
B. Create database backups
C. Tune indexes automatically
D. Replicate databases globally

Answer: A. Control which IP addresses can access the logical server
Reasoning:
Azure SQL firewall rules control network access to Azure SQL logical servers by allowing specific client IP ranges. Without an allowed IP or private endpoint configuration, clients cannot connect. Server-level firewall rules apply to all databases on the logical server, while database-level rules apply to specific databases. Firewall rules are a basic security control but should be combined with private endpoints, authentication, and least privilege permissions. They do not perform backup, tuning, or replication functions.

Q17. Which network feature allows private connectivity to Azure SQL over a virtual network?

A. Private Endpoint
B. Public IP only
C. Azure CDN

D. Traffic Manager

Answer: A. Private Endpoint
Reasoning:
Private Endpoint enables private connectivity to Azure SQL through Azure Private Link. It maps a private IP address from a virtual network to the Azure SQL service, allowing traffic to stay on the Microsoft backbone instead of using public internet access. This improves security by reducing public exposure. Public firewall access may be disabled when private endpoints are used. Azure CDN and Traffic Manager are not used for private SQL connectivity. DP-300 scenarios often test secure network access design.

Q18. Which feature should you use to monitor Azure SQL query performance over time?

A. Query Store
B. Azure DNS
C. Blob lifecycle management
D. Private DNS only

Answer: A. Query Store
Reasoning:
Query Store captures query text, execution plans, runtime statistics, and performance history. It helps identify plan regressions, expensive queries, and performance changes over time. DBAs can use it to compare plans and force a previous stable plan when needed. Azure SQL uses Query Store for several intelligent performance features. DNS and storage lifecycle features are unrelated to query performance. For DP-300, Query Store is central to troubleshooting and performance optimization tasks.

Q19. Which Azure SQL feature can automatically create or drop indexes based on workload patterns?

A. Automatic tuning
B. SQL auditing
C. Dynamic Data Masking
D. Geo-restore

Answer: A. Automatic tuning
Reasoning:
Automatic tuning in Azure SQL can apply recommendations such as creating indexes, dropping unused indexes, and forcing the last known good query plan. It uses intelligence from workload patterns and Query Store data. This can improve performance and reduce manual tuning effort. However, DBAs should still monitor recommendations and understand workload impact. Auditing tracks activity, masking protects output, and geo-restore recovers databases. Automatic tuning is part of Azure SQL intelligent performance capabilities.

Q20. What is the purpose of the Query Performance Insight feature?

A. Identify top resource-consuming queries
B. Create users
C. Configure firewall rules
D. Encrypt database files

Answer: A. Identify top resource-consuming queries
Reasoning:
Query Performance Insight helps identify queries consuming the most CPU, duration, or execution resources in Azure SQL Database. It provides visual performance analysis based on Query Store data. DBAs use it to find problematic queries and prioritize tuning efforts. It does not create users, configure networking, or encrypt files. For DP-300, performance troubleshooting often requires identifying bottlenecks, analyzing wait stats, reviewing execution plans, and using Query Store or Query Performance Insight.

Q21. Which command is commonly used to update statistics in SQL Server or Azure SQL?

A. UPDATE STATISTICS
B. CREATE LOGIN
C. BACKUP CERTIFICATE
D. ALTER FIREWALL

Answer: A. UPDATE STATISTICS
Reasoning:
Statistics help the SQL optimizer estimate row counts and choose efficient execution plans. Outdated statistics can lead to poor plans and slow queries. The UPDATE STATISTICS command refreshes statistics on tables or indexes. Azure SQL also has automatic statistics features, but DBAs may manually update statistics after large data changes. CREATE LOGIN manages security, BACKUP CERTIFICATE handles certificates, and ALTER FIREWALL is not the relevant SQL tuning command. Understanding statistics is important for DP-300 performance optimization.

Q22. Which index type is generally best for analytical queries scanning large tables?

A. Clustered columnstore index
B. Heap only
C. XML index only
D. Spatial index only

Answer: A. Clustered columnstore index
Reasoning:
Clustered columnstore indexes store data by columns instead of rows and provide high compression with efficient batch-mode processing. They are excellent for analytical workloads that scan, aggregate, and filter large datasets. Rowstore indexes are often better for OLTP point lookups and frequent small updates. XML and spatial indexes support specialized data types. For DP-300, choosing the right indexing strategy depends on workload type: OLTP usually benefits from selective rowstore indexes, while analytics often benefits from columnstore indexes.

Q23. What does Azure SQL Intelligent Insights help with?

A. Detecting database performance issues automatically
B. Creating DNS zones
C. Managing virtual machines
D. Replacing encryption

Answer: A. Detecting database performance issues automatically
Reasoning:
Intelligent Insights uses built-in intelligence to detect performance problems in Azure SQL Database and Managed Instance. It can identify issues such as increased waits, plan regressions, missing indexes, or workload changes. The goal is to help DBAs diagnose performance problems faster. It does not manage DNS, VMs, or encryption. In DP-300, monitoring and optimization include using Azure Monitor, Query Store, Intelligent Insights, wait statistics, and performance recommendations.

Q24. Which metric is most useful for identifying CPU pressure in Azure SQL Database?

A. CPU percentage
B. Database name
C. Firewall rule count
D. Tag count

Answer: A. CPU percentage
Reasoning:
CPU percentage indicates how much compute capacity the database is using. Sustained high CPU can show that the workload needs query tuning, indexing improvements, or scaling to a higher compute tier. It should be analyzed with other metrics like DTU/vCore usage, waits, deadlocks, and query performance data. Database name, firewall rules, and tags are not performance metrics. DP-300 candidates must know how to interpret Azure SQL metrics and decide whether to tune workload or scale resources.

Q25. Which Azure service is commonly used to collect and analyze Azure SQL logs and metrics?

A. Azure Monitor
B. Azure DNS
C. Azure Container Registry
D. Azure DevTest Labs

Answer: A. Azure Monitor
Reasoning:
Azure Monitor collects metrics, diagnostic logs, and activity logs from Azure resources, including Azure SQL. It can send data to Log Analytics for querying, dashboards, alerts, and deeper analysis. DBAs can monitor CPU, storage, deadlocks, failed connections, waits, and

auditing data. Azure DNS manages name resolution, Container Registry stores container images, and DevTest Labs manages test environments. DP-300 administrators should understand how to configure diagnostic settings and alerts for database resources.

Q26. Which feature allows Azure SQL Database to pause automatically when inactive?

A. Serverless compute tier
B. Business Critical tier
C. SQL Agent
D. Geo-replication

Answer: A. Serverless compute tier
Reasoning:
The serverless compute tier in Azure SQL Database can automatically scale compute based on workload and pause during inactivity, depending on configuration. This can reduce costs for intermittent or unpredictable workloads. When activity resumes, the database automatically resumes, although there may be a delay. Business Critical is always provisioned for high performance. SQL Agent handles job automation in Managed Instance and SQL Server, not database pausing. Serverless is mainly a cost optimization and elasticity feature for suitable workloads.

Q27. Which Azure SQL feature provides built-in automated backups?

A. Azure SQL Database default backup service
B. Manual export only
C. Azure DNS
D. Network Security Groups

Answer: A. Azure SQL Database default backup service
Reasoning:
Azure SQL Database automatically performs full, differential, and transaction log backups. These backups support point-in-time restore within the configured retention period. This is a managed PaaS capability and reduces the need for manual backup administration. Long-term retention can also be configured for compliance. Manual export is not a replacement for automated backups. DNS and NSGs are unrelated. DP-300 candidates must understand backup retention, point-in-time restore, long-term retention, and geo-restore options.

Q28. What is Point-in-Time Restore used for?

A. Restoring a database to a specific time within retention
B. Creating firewall rules
C. Encrypting columns
D. Scaling compute

Answer: A. Restoring a database to a specific time within retention
Reasoning:

Point-in-Time Restore (PITR) lets administrators restore an Azure SQL database to a specific moment within the backup retention period. It is useful after accidental deletes, incorrect updates, or data corruption. Azure SQL automated backups make PITR possible. The restore creates a new database rather than overwriting the existing one. Firewall, encryption, and compute scaling are separate administrative tasks. For DP-300, backup and restore scenarios are important in operational recovery and business continuity planning.

Q29. Which feature provides disaster recovery by replicating Azure SQL Database to another region?

A. Active geo-replication
B. Dynamic Data Masking
C. Query Store
D. SQL Auditing

Answer: A. Active geo-replication
Reasoning:
Active geo-replication creates readable secondary replicas of an Azure SQL Database in different regions. It is used for disaster recovery and read scale-out scenarios. If the primary region fails, administrators can fail over to a secondary database. Dynamic Data Masking protects query output, Query Store monitors performance, and Auditing records activity. DP-300 HA/DR questions often compare active geo-replication, failover groups, zone redundancy, backups, and geo-restore.

Q30. What is the purpose of auto-failover groups in Azure SQL?

A. Manage failover for multiple databases together
B. Create local users
C. Compress indexes
D. Mask query output

Answer: A. Manage failover for multiple databases together
Reasoning:
Auto-failover groups simplify disaster recovery by allowing one or more databases to fail over together to a secondary server in another region. They provide listener endpoints for read-write and read-only workloads, making application connection management easier during failover. Compared with configuring individual geo-replication, failover groups are better for applications with multiple related databases. They do not manage users, indexes, or data masking. DP-300 administrators must understand failover policies, grace periods, and application connection considerations.

Q31. Which Azure SQL feature allows read-only workloads to be offloaded to secondary replicas?

A. Read scale-out
B. Data masking
C. Auditing
D. Firewall rules

Answer: A. Read scale-out
Reasoning:
Read scale-out enables applications to send read-only queries to secondary replicas instead of the primary database. This improves performance by reducing load on the primary instance, especially in read-heavy workloads like reporting or analytics. It is supported in Business Critical and Hyperscale tiers. This feature enhances scalability and availability without affecting transactional workloads. It does not relate to security or networking features like masking or firewall rules. Understanding workload separation is important for performance optimization in DP-300.

Q32. What is the purpose of database failover groups listener endpoint?

A. Manage DNS records
B. Provide a single connection endpoint for failover
C. Store backups
D. Encrypt data

Answer: B
Reasoning:
Failover group listeners provide a stable DNS endpoint that applications use to connect to databases. When failover occurs, the listener automatically redirects connections to the new primary database, eliminating the need to update connection strings. This simplifies application design and improves resilience. It supports both read-write and read-only endpoints. Listener endpoints are essential in disaster recovery strategies and are widely tested in DP-300 scenarios.

Q33. Which backup type captures only changes since the last full backup?

A. Full backup
B. Differential backup
C. Transaction log backup
D. Snapshot backup

Answer: B
Reasoning:
Differential backups store only the changes made since the last full backup, making them faster and smaller. They help reduce recovery time by minimizing the number of backups needed during restore operations. Transaction log backups capture incremental changes at a finer level,

but differential backups balance size and speed. Azure SQL automates these processes, but understanding backup types is critical for planning recovery strategies.

Q34. What is the purpose of transaction log backups?

A. Store full data
B. Capture incremental changes
C. Encrypt database
D. Monitor queries

Answer: B
Reasoning:
Transaction log backups capture all changes made to the database since the last log backup. They allow point-in-time recovery and help minimize data loss. In Azure SQL, log backups are taken automatically. Understanding log backups is important for recovery planning, especially in mission-critical systems where minimizing downtime and data loss is essential.

Q35. Which Azure SQL feature supports long-term backup retention?

A. LTR (Long-Term Retention)
B. Elastic pool
C. Query Store
D. Firewall

Answer: A
Reasoning:
Long-Term Retention (LTR) allows storing backups for months or years for compliance or auditing purposes. It is useful in industries with strict regulatory requirements. LTR backups are stored separately from short-term backups used for point-in-time restore. This ensures historical data can be retrieved even long after normal retention periods expire.

Q36. What is geo-restore used for?

A. Local recovery
B. Restore database in another region
C. Encrypt database
D. Scale compute

Answer: B
Reasoning:
Geo-restore allows restoring a database from geo-redundant backups in another Azure region. It is used when the primary region is unavailable due to a major outage. This feature ensures business continuity but may involve some data loss depending on backup timing. It is different from active geo-replication, which provides near real-time replication.

Q37. What is the purpose of SQL Server Agent (in Managed Instance)?

A. Backup
B. Schedule jobs and automation tasks
C. Encrypt data
D. Manage DNS

Answer: B
Reasoning:
SQL Server Agent allows scheduling jobs such as backups, maintenance tasks, and scripts. It is available in SQL Server and Azure SQL Managed Instance but not in Azure SQL Database. It helps automate repetitive tasks, improving efficiency and reliability.

Q38. Which feature tracks query execution plans over time?

A. Query Store
B. Azure Policy
C. Azure Backup
D. Azure Firewall

Answer: A
Reasoning:
Query Store records execution plans and performance statistics over time. It helps identify performance regressions and allows DBAs to force stable plans. This feature is essential for troubleshooting performance issues in Azure SQL environments.

Q39. What is index fragmentation?

A. Encryption
B. Disorganized data pages in index
C. Backup issue
D. Network issue

Answer: B
Reasoning:
Index fragmentation occurs when data pages are not stored sequentially, leading to inefficient disk access. It can degrade query performance. DBAs use index rebuild or reorganize operations to fix fragmentation. Understanding index maintenance is crucial for DP-300.

Q40. Which command rebuilds an index?

A. ALTER INDEX REBUILD
B. DROP INDEX
C. CREATE TABLE
D. UPDATE LOGIN

Answer: A

Reasoning:
ALTER INDEX REBUILD reorganizes the entire index, removing fragmentation and improving performance. It is more resource-intensive than reorganize but provides better results. DBAs must choose between rebuild and reorganize based on fragmentation level.

Q41. What is deadlock in SQL Server?

A. Backup failure
B. Two processes blocking each other
C. Encryption issue
D. Network error

Answer: B
Reasoning:
A deadlock occurs when two transactions wait on each other's resources, causing both to stop. SQL Server resolves deadlocks by terminating one process. Monitoring and resolving deadlocks is important for database stability.

Q42. Which tool helps detect deadlocks in Azure SQL?

A. Azure Monitor
B. Azure DNS
C. Azure Files
D. Azure Backup

Answer: A
Reasoning:
Azure Monitor collects logs and metrics that help identify deadlocks. Query Store also helps analyze such issues. Monitoring tools are essential for troubleshooting database problems.

Q43. What is DTU model based on?

A. Separate CPU and memory
B. Combined performance units
C. Storage only
D. Network only

Answer: B
Reasoning:
DTU combines CPU, memory, and I/O into a single performance unit. It simplifies sizing but provides less flexibility than vCore model.

Q44. What is vCore model advantage?

A. Simplicity
B. Flexibility and control

C. Free storage
D. No backup

Answer: B
Reasoning:
vCore model allows independent scaling of compute and storage, making it more flexible and transparent.

Q45. What is tempdb used for?

A. Permanent storage
B. Temporary objects and operations
C. Backup
D. Encryption

Answer: B
Reasoning:
tempdb stores temporary data such as temp tables, sorting operations, and intermediate results.

Q46. What is Azure SQL serverless auto-pause feature?

A. Deletes database
B. Stops compute when idle
C. Encrypts data
D. Backup

Answer: B
Reasoning:
Auto-pause reduces cost by stopping compute resources when database is inactive.

Q47. What is database collation?

A. Backup setting
B. Rules for sorting and comparing data
C. Encryption
D. Networking

Answer: B
Reasoning:
Collation defines how text is sorted and compared, including case sensitivity.

Q48. What is parameter sniffing issue?

A. Backup problem
B. Query plan issue based on parameter values
C. Encryption problem

D. DNS issue

Answer: B
Reasoning:
Parameter sniffing occurs when SQL Server uses a cached plan that may not be optimal for all parameter values.

Q49. What is purpose of indexing?

A. Backup
B. Improve query performance
C. Encrypt data
D. Monitor logs

Answer: B
Reasoning:
Indexes speed up data retrieval by allowing faster search operations.

Q50. What is clustered index?

A. Separate storage
B. Defines physical order of data
C. Backup
D. Encryption

Answer: B
Reasoning:
Clustered index determines how data is physically stored in the table.

Q51–60 (Short + reasoning)

Q51: Non-clustered index → Separate structure for faster lookup
Q52: Covering index → Includes all needed columns
Q53: Statistics → Help optimizer choose plan
Q54: Wait stats → Identify performance bottlenecks
Q55: CPU bottleneck → High CPU usage
Q56: I/O bottleneck → Slow disk operations
Q57: Memory pressure → Insufficient memory
Q58: Query plan → Execution strategy
Q59: Execution plan analysis → Optimize queries
Q60: Performance tuning → Improve efficiency

Q61. What is the purpose of execution plans in SQL Server?

A. Backup database
B. Show how queries are executed
C. Manage firewall
D. Encrypt data

Answer: B
Reasoning:
Execution plans describe how SQL Server processes a query, including operations like scans, joins, and sorts. They help DBAs understand performance issues and optimize queries. By analyzing execution plans, you can identify inefficient operations such as table scans or missing indexes. This is essential in DP-300 for troubleshooting slow queries and improving performance. Execution plans do not manage backups, security, or networking, but they are critical for query tuning and optimization.

Q62. What is a table scan?

A. Using index
B. Reading entire table
C. Backup process
D. Encryption

Answer: B
Reasoning:
A table scan occurs when SQL Server reads all rows in a table to find the required data. This is inefficient for large tables and often indicates missing indexes. DBAs aim to replace table scans with index seeks for better performance. Understanding scans vs seeks is important for query optimization in DP-300.

Q63. What is an index seek?

A. Full table read
B. Efficient search using index
C. Backup method
D. Encryption

Answer: B
Reasoning:
Index seek uses an index to quickly locate specific rows, improving performance compared to scans. It is ideal for selective queries and is a key indicator of efficient query execution.

Q64. What is cardinality estimation?

A. Backup size
B. Estimate number of rows returned

C. Encryption level
D. Network latency

Answer: B
Reasoning:
Cardinality estimation helps SQL Server predict how many rows a query will return. Accurate estimates lead to better execution plans. Poor estimation can cause inefficient queries.

Q65. What is parameterization in SQL?

A. Backup
B. Replacing values with parameters
C. Encryption
D. Networking

Answer: B
Reasoning:
Parameterization improves performance and security by reusing query plans and preventing SQL injection. It is important for scalable applications.

Q66. What is query plan caching?

A. Backup
B. Storing execution plans for reuse
C. Encryption
D. DNS

Answer: B
Reasoning:
SQL Server caches execution plans to avoid recompiling queries repeatedly. This improves performance but can cause issues like parameter sniffing.

Q67. What is plan forcing?

A. Backup
B. Forcing a specific execution plan
C. Encryption
D. DNS

Answer: B
Reasoning:
Plan forcing ensures a stable execution plan is used, preventing performance regressions caused by plan changes.

Q68. What is Azure SQL automatic tuning force plan?

A. Backup
B. Automatically enforce best plan
C. Encryption
D. DNS

Answer: B
Reasoning:
Automatic tuning can force a known good plan to improve performance automatically.

Q69. What is CPU wait type?

A. Backup
B. Time spent waiting for CPU
C. Encryption
D. DNS

Answer: B
Reasoning:
Wait statistics help identify performance bottlenecks. CPU waits indicate processing delays.

Q70. What is I/O wait?

A. Backup
B. Delay in disk operations
C. Encryption
D. DNS

Answer: B
Reasoning:
I/O waits indicate slow storage performance, affecting query execution.

Q71. What is memory grant?

A. Backup
B. Memory allocated for query execution
C. Encryption
D. DNS

Answer: B
Reasoning:
Memory grants ensure queries have enough memory for operations like sorting and joining.

Q72. What is tempdb contention?

A. Backup issue
B. High usage causing performance issues

C. Encryption
D. DNS

Answer: B
Reasoning:
tempdb contention occurs when multiple processes compete for tempdb resources, affecting performance.

Q73. What is deadlock priority?

A. Backup
B. Determines which process is killed
C. Encryption
D. DNS

Answer: B
Reasoning:
Deadlock priority decides which transaction is terminated during a deadlock.

Q74. What is lock escalation?

A. Backup
B. Converting many locks into fewer locks
C. Encryption
D. DNS

Answer: B
Reasoning:
Lock escalation reduces overhead by consolidating locks but may increase blocking.

Q75. What is blocking?

A. Backup
B. One query waiting for another
C. Encryption
D. DNS

Answer: B
Reasoning:
Blocking occurs when one transaction holds a lock needed by another.

Q76. What is isolation level?

A. Backup
B. Controls transaction visibility
C. Encryption

D. DNS

Answer: B
Reasoning:
Isolation levels define how transactions interact, affecting consistency and concurrency.

Q77. What is READ COMMITTED?

A. Backup
B. Prevents dirty reads
C. Encryption
D. DNS

Answer: B
Reasoning:
READ COMMITTED ensures only committed data is read.

Q78. What is snapshot isolation?

A. Backup
B. Uses versioning to avoid blocking
C. Encryption
D. DNS

Answer: B
Reasoning:
Snapshot isolation reduces blocking by using row versioning.

Q79. What is dirty read?

A. Backup
B. Reading uncommitted data
C. Encryption
D. DNS

Answer: B
Reasoning:
Dirty reads can lead to inconsistent results.

Q80. What is phantom read?

A. Backup
B. Rows appearing/disappearing during transaction
C. Encryption
D. DNS

Answer: B
Reasoning:
Phantom reads occur when new rows appear during a transaction.

Q81–90 (Short + reasoning)

Q81: ACID → Transaction reliability principles
Q82: Atomicity → All or nothing execution
Q83: Consistency → Valid state maintained
Q84: Isolation → Transactions independent
Q85: Durability → Changes persist after commit
Q86: Checkpoint → Writes data to disk
Q87: Log file → Stores transaction history
Q88: Recovery model → Controls logging behavior
Q89: Full recovery → Supports point-in-time restore
Q90: Simple recovery → Minimal logging

Q91. What is the FULL recovery model used for?

A. Minimal logging
B. Point-in-time recovery
C. No backups
D. Faster queries

Answer: B
Reasoning:
The FULL recovery model records all transactions in the transaction log, enabling point-in-time recovery. This is essential for critical systems where data loss must be minimized. It requires regular transaction log backups to prevent the log file from growing too large. Compared to SIMPLE recovery, FULL provides better data protection but requires more management. DP-300 focuses on choosing the correct recovery model based on business requirements.

Q92. What is SIMPLE recovery model?

A. Full logging
B. Minimal logging without log backups
C. Encryption
D. Monitoring

Answer: B
Reasoning:
SIMPLE recovery model automatically truncates the transaction log, reducing administrative overhead. However, it does not support point-in-time recovery. It is suitable for non-critical systems where some data loss is acceptable.

Q93. What is BULK LOGGED recovery model?

A. No logging
B. Minimal logging for bulk operations
C. Encryption
D. DNS

Answer: B
Reasoning:
BULK LOGGED reduces log usage during bulk operations like bulk inserts. It balances performance and recoverability but does not support full point-in-time recovery during bulk operations.

Q94. What is database mirroring replaced by?

A. Geo-replication
B. Failover groups
C. Backup

D. DNS

Answer: B
Reasoning:
Database mirroring is deprecated and replaced by modern solutions like failover groups and Always On availability groups.

Q95. What is Always On Availability Groups?

A. Backup
B. High availability and disaster recovery solution
C. Encryption
D. DNS

Answer: B
Reasoning:
Always On Availability Groups provide HA/DR by replicating databases across multiple servers. It supports automatic failover and read-only replicas.

Q96. What is failover?

A. Backup
B. Switching to secondary system during failure
C. Encryption
D. DNS

Answer: B
Reasoning:
Failover ensures system continuity when the primary system fails.

Q97. What is failback?

A. Backup
B. Returning to primary after recovery
C. Encryption
D. DNS

Answer: B
Reasoning:
Failback restores operations to the original system after recovery.

Q98. What is RPO (Recovery Point Objective)?

A. Backup time
B. Maximum acceptable data loss
C. Encryption

D. DNS

Answer: B
Reasoning:
RPO defines how much data loss is acceptable during a failure.

Q99. What is RTO (Recovery Time Objective)?

A. Backup size
B. Maximum acceptable downtime
C. Encryption
D. DNS

Answer: B
Reasoning:
RTO defines how quickly systems must be restored.

Q100. What is zone redundancy?

A. Backup
B. Replication across availability zones
C. Encryption
D. DNS

Answer: B
Reasoning:
Zone redundancy ensures data availability across physically separate datacenters.

Q101. What is Azure SQL failover group policy?

A. Backup
B. Controls automatic failover behavior
C. Encryption
D. DNS

Answer: B
Reasoning:
Failover policies define how and when failover occurs automatically.

Q102. What is manual failover?

A. Backup
B. Admin-triggered failover
C. Encryption
D. DNS

Answer: B
Reasoning:
Manual failover is initiated by administrators when needed.

Q103. What is read-only replica?

A. Backup
B. Secondary database for read queries
C. Encryption
D. DNS

Answer: B
Reasoning:
Read-only replicas improve performance by handling read workloads.

Q104. What is Azure SQL backup redundancy?

A. Storage only
B. LRS, ZRS, GRS options
C. Encryption
D. DNS

Answer: B
Reasoning:
Backup redundancy determines how backups are replicated for durability.

Q105. What is backup retention policy?

A. Storage
B. Duration backups are stored
C. Encryption
D. DNS

Answer: B
Reasoning:
Retention policy defines how long backups are kept.

Q106. What is database restore operation?

A. Backup
B. Recovering database from backup
C. Encryption
D. DNS

Answer: B
Reasoning:

Restore operations recover databases after failure or data loss.

Q107. What is copy database?

A. Backup
B. Creating duplicate database
C. Encryption
D. DNS

Answer: B
Reasoning:
Copy database creates a separate instance of database.

Q108. What is export database?

A. Backup
B. Export to BACPAC file
C. Encryption
D. DNS

Answer: B
Reasoning:
Export creates a portable file for migration or backup.

Q109. What is import database?

A. Backup
B. Import from BACPAC
C. Encryption
D. DNS

Answer: B
Reasoning:
Import restores database from exported file.

Q110. What is Azure SQL auditing log retention?

A. Storage
B. Duration logs are kept
C. Encryption
D. DNS

Answer: B
Reasoning:
Audit logs are retained based on configured policies.

Q111–120 (Short + reasoning)

Q111: Encryption key → Protect data
Q112: Certificate → Used for encryption
Q113: Transparent encryption → Protect data at rest
Q114: TLS → Encrypt data in transit
Q115: Firewall → Control access
Q116: Private endpoint → Secure access
Q117: RBAC → Access control
Q118: Identity → Authentication
Q119: Compliance → Meet regulations
Q120: Governance → Manage policies

Q121. What is the purpose of Azure SQL auditing logs destination?

A. Backup storage
B. Store audit logs in Storage, Log Analytics, or Event Hub
C. Encrypt database
D. Manage users

Answer: B
Reasoning:
Azure SQL Auditing allows sending logs to multiple destinations such as Azure Storage (for long-term retention), Log Analytics (for querying and analysis), and Event Hub (for integration with external SIEM systems). Choosing the right destination depends on compliance, monitoring, and integration needs. For example, Log Analytics is ideal for querying audit data using KQL, while Storage is better for archival. Understanding log destinations is important in DP-300 for designing monitoring and compliance solutions.

Q122. What is the purpose of Log Analytics workspace?

A. Store backups
B. Central place to analyze logs and metrics
C. Encrypt data
D. Manage DNS

Answer: B
Reasoning:
Log Analytics workspace is a central repository used by Azure Monitor to collect, store, and analyze logs from multiple Azure resources. It allows querying data using KQL, building dashboards, and creating alerts. For Azure SQL, it is commonly used for auditing logs, performance metrics, and diagnostics. It does not handle backups or encryption but plays a key role in monitoring and troubleshooting.

Q123. What is KQL (Kusto Query Language)?

A. Backup script
B. Query language for Log Analytics
C. Encryption tool
D. DNS command

Answer: B
Reasoning:
KQL is used to query data stored in Azure Monitor and Log Analytics. It helps analyze logs, detect anomalies, and create reports. DBAs use KQL to troubleshoot performance issues, monitor activity, and detect security threats. It is not used for encryption or DNS management.

Q124. What is Azure SQL Intelligent Performance?

A. Backup feature
B. Automated performance tuning and insights
C. Encryption
D. DNS

Answer: B
Reasoning:
Azure SQL Intelligent Performance includes features like Query Store, Automatic Tuning, and Intelligent Insights. These tools help identify and resolve performance issues automatically. They reduce manual effort and improve database efficiency. DP-300 requires understanding how to use these tools for optimization.

Q125. What is the purpose of WAIT statistics?

A. Backup
B. Identify resource bottlenecks
C. Encryption
D. DNS

Answer: B
Reasoning:
WAIT statistics show where SQL Server spends time waiting for resources such as CPU, I/O, or locks. Analyzing waits helps identify performance bottlenecks. For example, high I/O waits indicate disk issues. DP-300 emphasizes performance troubleshooting using wait stats.

Q126. What is Azure SQL resource governance?

A. Backup
B. Control resource usage per workload
C. Encryption
D. DNS

Answer: B
Reasoning:
Resource governance ensures workloads do not consume excessive resources, maintaining stability and fairness. It helps manage CPU, memory, and I/O usage.

Q127. What is workload classification?

A. Backup
B. Categorizing queries for resource management
C. Encryption
D. DNS

Answer: B
Reasoning:

Workload classification assigns workloads to resource groups for better performance control.

Q128. What is query hint?

A. Backup
B. Instruction to optimizer
C. Encryption
D. DNS

Answer: B
Reasoning:
Query hints influence execution plans, helping optimize performance.

Q129. What is parameterized query advantage?

A. Backup
B. Improves plan reuse and security
C. Encryption
D. DNS

Answer: B
Reasoning:
Parameterized queries reduce compilation overhead and prevent SQL injection.

Q130. What is database compatibility level?

A. Backup
B. Controls behavior of SQL features
C. Encryption
D. DNS

Answer: B
Reasoning:
Compatibility level determines how SQL Server interprets queries and features, ensuring backward compatibility.

Q131. What is Azure SQL scaling?

A. Backup
B. Increasing/decreasing resources
C. Encryption
D. DNS

Answer: B
Reasoning:
Scaling adjusts compute and storage based on workload demand.

Q132. What is vertical scaling?

A. Backup
B. Increase resources of single instance
C. Encryption
D. DNS

Answer: B
Reasoning:
Vertical scaling increases CPU, memory, or storage.

Q133. What is horizontal scaling?

A. Backup
B. Add more instances
C. Encryption
D. DNS

Answer: B
Reasoning:
Horizontal scaling distributes load across multiple instances.

Q134. What is read scale-out scenario?

A. Backup
B. Offload reads to replicas
C. Encryption
D. DNS

Answer: B
Reasoning:
Improves performance by separating read and write workloads.

Q135. What is database sharding?

A. Backup
B. Splitting data across databases
C. Encryption
D. DNS

Answer: B
Reasoning:
Sharding improves scalability by distributing data.

Q136. What is Azure SQL elasticity?

A. Backup
B. Automatic scaling capability
C. Encryption
D. DNS

Answer: B
Reasoning:
Elasticity allows resources to adjust automatically.

Q137. What is throttling in Azure SQL?

A. Backup
B. Limiting resource usage
C. Encryption
D. DNS

Answer: B
Reasoning:
Throttling occurs when resource limits are exceeded.

Q138. What is DTU utilization metric?

A. Backup
B. Measures resource consumption
C. Encryption
D. DNS

Answer: B
Reasoning:
DTU shows combined CPU, memory, and I/O usage.

Q139. What is vCore utilization?

A. Backup
B. Measures CPU usage
C. Encryption
D. DNS

Answer: B
Reasoning:
vCore metrics track CPU performance.

Q140. What is database latency?

A. Backup

B. Delay in query response
C. Encryption
D. DNS

Answer: B
Reasoning:
Latency affects user experience and performance.

Q141–150 (Short + reasoning)

Q141: Index maintenance → Improve performance
Q142: Fragmentation → Disorganized index
Q143: Rebuild vs reorganize → Fix fragmentation
Q144: Query optimization → Improve speed
Q145: Execution plan analysis → Identify issues
Q146: Monitoring → Track performance
Q147: Alerts → Notify issues
Q148: Automation → Reduce manual work
Q149: Backup strategy → Ensure recovery
Q150: DR planning → Ensure business continuity

YouTube Link for Viva Voce Questions:
https://www.youtube.com/playlist?list=PLzlh_31VWEFo5GZsiCvrVVnOL-ol_Lg-c

QR Code:

YouTube Videos Playlists for all Microsoft Certifications Videos

Microsoft Azure AI Fundamentals AZ-900
Link: https://www.youtube.com/playlist?list=PLzlh_31VWEFq9KU8Gr0ISbfj-TW6k17f8

QR Code:

Microsoft Azure Administrator AZ-104 Microsoft Azure Virtual Desktop AZ-140
Link: https://www.youtube.com/playlist?list=PLzlh_31VWEFq7JHJMuPJZcw-XShaPrUYP

QR Code:

Microsoft Azure Virtual Desktop AZ-140
Link: https://www.youtube.com/playlist?list=PLzlh_31VWEFowmPK_ro41wiljGoGKexGI

QR Code:

Microsoft Azure Developer AZ-204
Link:
https://www.youtube.com/playlist?list=PLzlh_31VWEFqT72UPVCUi6rqRqLBuwMSr

QR Code:

Designing Microsoft Azure Infrastructure Solution AZ-305
Link:
https://www.youtube.com/playlist?list=PLzlh_31VWEFpTerOknh9kgL4eTbhQwDND

QR Code:

Microsoft Azure Devops Engineer AZ-400
Link: https://www.youtube.com/playlist?list=PLzlh_31VWEFpyUIe_DuaeIkcThEfMT_BT

QR Code:

Microsoft Azure Security Engineer AZ-500
Link:
https://www.youtube.com/playlist?list=PLzlh_31VWEFqFBJgQTPNucIO0wVJdjNmS

QR Code:

Microsoft Azure Network Engineer AZ-700
Link:
https://www.youtube.com/playlist?list=PLzlh_31VWEFowujgDl16YDCvsQtmKgEqL

QR Code:

Microsoft Azure Fundamentals AZ-900
Link: https://www.youtube.com/playlist?list=PLzlh_31VWEFpeXZ2p32R1zDsgcbV8kI1K

QR Code:

Microsoft Azure Data Engineer DP-203
Link: https://www.youtube.com/playlist?list=PLzlh_31VWEFp3XTNqoS60UAOzl8NVG-5z

QR Code:

Microsoft Azure Database Administrator DP- 300
Link: https://www.youtube.com/playlist?list=PLzlh_31VWEFpv-rmc2mbpoIqUOqVW_cIo

QR Code: